Man on the Scene

By Jeff Quinn

Published in cooperation with Mutie publishing.

National Library of Canada Cataloguing in Publication

Quinn, Jeff, 1966-
     Man on the scene / Jeff Quinn.
ISBN 1-4120-1176-0
     I. Title.
G465.Q55 2004   910.4   C2003-904681-8

TRAFFORD

This book was published *on-demand* in cooperation with Trafford Publishing. On-demand publishing is a unique process and service of making a book available for retail sale to the public taking advantage of on-demand manufacturing and Internet marketing. **On-demand publishing** includes promotions, retail sales, manufacturing, order fulfilment, accounting and collecting royalties on behalf of the author.

Suite 6E, 2333 Government St., Victoria, B.C. V8T 4P4, CANADA
Phone   250-383-6864   Toll-free   1-888-232-4444 (Canada & US)
Fax   250-383-6804   E-mail   sales@trafford.com
Web site   www.trafford.com   TRAFFORD PUBLISHING IS A DIVISION OF TRAFFORD HOLDINGS LTD.
Trafford Catalogue #03-1553   www.trafford.com/robots/03-1553.html

10   9   8   7   6   5   4   3   2   1

Contents

Introduction

Welcome to Man on the Scene. Beware. This is my first crack at book writing, so there may be some blatant and heinous mistakes. I hope not, but when you self-edit a book, mistakes are bound to occur, thus the lame disclaimer.

This book chronicles a few of my adventures over the years. There are many more, but I'm afraid some of them are simply unprintable. Perhaps those tales are better told around a roaring campfire with fewer witnesses. The stories in this collection are fairly concise and to the point. Many of the characters (especially my own friends) are undeveloped. I'm afraid I tend to think rather fragmentally. Therefore, some of my sentences tend to be choppy fragments at times. They make sense to me and I can only hope they make sense to you.

I tried not to offend anyone, but if I did, I apologize. Sometimes my realistic nature cuts like a razor.

Travel has become an addiction for me. I constantly feel the need to plan and execute a new adventure. I try to always have a new one in the planning stages at all times. It gives me something to look forward to. And I'm the kind of person that always needs something to look forward to. Now if I could only do something about this aging thing.

"How the hell do you afford to go on these trips?", is probably the most frequently asked question that I field from people.

First of all, I travel on the cheap whenever possible. I find cheap airfares, stay at cheap hotels, and tend to travel to cheap or affordable locales, preferably third world or developing locales. I guess the bottom line is...I'm just a cheap bastard.

There always seems to be more going on in third world countries. Life in its rawest form. We take so much for granted in the United States. Travel really allows me to appreciate my own life. Traffic seems lighter, polluted air looks clearer and even food seems to taste better when I return home after a trip.

Secondly, I don't blow lots of cash every weekend at the bar and I tend to avoid the mall (like the plague) whenever possible. Two places that can definitely drain my already low budget in a hurry.

The next question people inevitably ask me is "why do you travel?". In response, I'd have to say that I just feel the need to see the world through my own eyes and experiences. I need to smell the smells and taste the tastes of a culture, may they happen to be pleasant or unpleasant. I need to feel the humidity of the rainforest in Malaysia and the high altitude lung-tug of the Andes. I like to self-educate. To learn new things. To meet new and different faces in crazy, distant places. I like to meet them, then suck their minds dry. I love to ask questions and I try to understand all that I can. Travel has allowed me to grow wiser and much more intelligent. Besides, it's fun as hell...Most of the time. Travel is also full of downtime and tough decisions. Most trips are a work in progress. You plan and adjust. And then you plan and adjust some more.

Finally, I'd like to thank my family and friends for all their fine support over the years. I couldn't have done it without them, especially my parents Edward and Reta Quinn.

In Search of Babalowas... And a Way to Beat the Embargo Blues

Cuba, 2003

If you want to go to Cuba...Legally...And you're an American, better prepare to jump through some hoops, but it'll be worth your while. I had a trip planned to visit my friend Dusty Decarlo in Florida over my spring break and I figured Cuba was so close, so why not? Ever since the 60s, the U.S. trade embargo against Cuba has prevented casual trips to the largest Caribbean Island by American tourists. That doesn't mean people don't go. Thousands visit Cuba each year by traveling through "third" countries en route to Cuba such as Mexico, Jamaica, or the Bahamas. The trick is to conceal the fact that you ever touched Cuban soil, denial being your best option. The Cubans won't stamp your passport, because they know you'll get into hot water with the U.S. customs authorities when you return to the States.

Being an honest upstanding citizen (perhaps next time I'll go illegally myself), I elected to follow the proper protocol and fly legally from Miami. I won't bore you with the amount of phone calls I had to make (too many to count) to a travel agency in Miami specializing in Cuban travel in order to obtain tickets. But, let's just say it took several months of negotiation and faxes, in order to procure a $300 round trip ticket from Miami to Havana. Buying the ticket was the easy part. Qualifying for the ticket was the hard part. Only travelers meeting strict guidelines can legally travel to Cuba. Immediate family members, professional athletes

(I thought they only left Cuba), missionaries on official business, full-time journalists, government cronies, researchers on assignment, and a slight few others that I can't quite recall at the moment.

I scratched my head and asked myself which category I might somehow qualify for? Well, I am a Geography and Sociology teacher, and I like to travel, write, take pictures, and ask questions, so I must be a researcher. There it was. Now I only had to figure out what the hell it was that I was supposed to be researching just in case I was asked to produce evidence.

I decided to research Santeria, which had always intrigued me. Santeria is a mixture of Catholicism and various African religions. I had read about locations throughout the greater Havana area where Santeria was openly practiced and had even read about markets specializing in Santeria products. As far as what those products might be...Well, that's another story altogether. I had visions of the movie *The Deep* running through my head.

I came up with a half-assed working itinerary (required by the United States Government) that included visits to Santeria sites and even lunch interviews with famous babalowas (Santeria priests who can be identified in Cuba by their green and yellow bracelets). I thought I might even call a clandestine dinner meeting with the Abakua, or secret men society in Regla?

Being a teacher, the research angle wasn't so far-fetched. I just had to figure out a way for my friend Dusty to get in. We decided that I would need an assistant, to help me research the Santeria clan. Someone that could help translate Spanish as well. Too bad Dusty's only Spanish word is Digame', or talk to me. Nevertheless, I added Dusty to my itinerary and after filling out and faxing more paperwork, we eventually received our tickets and tourist visas to Cuba. We had to personally pick up our tickets in Little Havana prior to departure. I guess that was a sneak preview or something.

4

Looking back, I think more Cubans live in Little Havana than Big Havana.

Dusty and I arrived at the Miami International Airport ready to depart for Havana. The flight was a whopping fifty minutes long. First off, we had to find the correct terminal. No easy task. We walked through each adjoining terminal until we came to the end of the airport, whereupon we asked a custodian where our terminal was located. "You're here", he answered. I said where? "Right here". Then we spotted a guy cellophane wrapping colorful luggage and we knew we were in the right spot. A line behind a card table told the tale. Here was the flight that really didn't exist. We were two out of only a handful of gringos traveling to Havana. Most were Cubans going home for a visit. You could tell us apart right away...Our backpacks were uncellophaned.

We arrived at Jose Marti International Airport in Havana after an uneventful flight. Luckily for us, the hijackers were leaving Cuba, not coming in. Strangely enough, a string of hijackings occurred the week after we arrived back in the States. Two planes and one boat were commandeered. Apparently the hijackers thought that if they arrived on United States soil after hijacking a plane they were allowed to stay based on the Dry Land Act. They weren't. Ironically, the hijacked passengers, who were forced to land by fighter jets in the Florida Keys were given the choice to stay in the U.S. or go home. The hijackers got to stay as well...In a U.S. federal prison. Castro figured it was a few less mouths to feed.

We pretty much breezed through customs after a few questions about why we were there and most importantly, when we were leaving. Official business, I told them, serious research. They didn't ask Dusty anything. All we had were daypacks with us, so the customs officials had nothing much to do. I sensed they liked it that way. Why bother an hombre on siesta with trivialities?

We finally managed to track down a ride into

the city as our contact failed to show.
Fortunately, one of the other travel agencies
set us up with transportation. I always look
forward to that initial cab ride in any new
place I venture to. So many sights to behold.
My senses just go wild...I can't get enough.
Everything is similar and different all at the
same time. Everyday, ordinary occurrences
appear so bizarre to an outsider looking in.
After about thirty or forty minutes we arrived
at the Hotel Lincoln.

In order to obtain our visa, we had to
procure hotel reservations in advance. I'm
pretty damned cheap when I travel, so luxury
accommodations are generally avoided...Like the
plague. Besides, it's way more authentic
hanging out in cheaper hotels. The cheaper the
better. I figure I'm only sleeping there, so it
doesn't need to be very extravagant. As long as
it doesn't have bugs...Or at least not too many
of them. Hot water is generally a luxury that
we go without. Not on purpose of course...And a
definite bonus when it appears...Only to
suddenly disappear as fast as it had appeared.

Anyway, long story short, I had originally
arranged for a place called Hotel New York,
which must have been so cheap that it didn't
appear on the rolls at the travel agency, so I
opted for my second choice: The Hotel Lincoln.
We expected a real dump, but surprisingly enough
the place was actually pretty nice. A small
fourth floor balcony view of the ocean down the
street and the people doing their thing on the
street below. Running water, two beds, and
cable television...What else could a guy want?
Hell, it was ten times better than the run-down
shanty we stayed in the previous night in the
Keys. And you guessed it...Cheaper. I figured
that if it was good enough for the Cuban World
Series participants (they were in the lobby as
we checked in), that it was good enough for me.
I wondered how my beloved Diamondbacks would
have embraced these digs?

We were centrally located in La Habana Viejo
or Old Havana. The area lived up to its ageism.

It definitely didn't resemble anything new.
Run-down streets and dilapidated buildings have
a certain charm. A certain ambiance. Besides,
if I wanted to avoid Cubans, I would have stayed
in Varadero, where Cubans are prohibited in
their own country. Only tourists and hookers.
Why bother? Might as well go to Club Med or a
time-share in St. Thomas. No, it really is the
people that I enjoy. I love meeting and
learning about different cultures and look
forward to meeting new friends from another
land. And my ex-wife says I'm unsociable.

Probably the first thing that anyone notices
upon arrival in Havana are the rides. If you
like vintage Chevrolets, Fords, and Chryslers,
then you're in the right place. It's like
taking a time machine back to the 1950s. The
old cars are everywhere. Since the embargo in
the early 1960s, American cars have been
unavailable in Cuba; thus everybody keeps these
old relics rolling down the road. Kind of
anyway. You can almost pinpoint the date of the
embargo by the year of the cars. There are also
quite a few Russian Ladas and some Japanese
cars. The streets are fairly uncongested due to
the embargo. Probably the least car-congested
Latin American country in the world.

After checking out the facilities at the
Hotel Lincoln, which included flushing the
toilet and looking in the mirror, we were off to
explore Havana. Heading east, we hoofed it down
narrow streets and alleyways through the
tropical midday humidity. We were only walking
for about twenty or thirty minutes when we ran
into Otuardo. I can't really remember exactly
what was said, but he answered a question in
English that I had posed to Dusty and soon after
we were hanging out. At the time of our
encounter, he had been out on a walk with his
wife and one of their children. Otuardo and his
wife were both physicians. He told us that he
made $21 a month. Less than a waiter at the
cantina. And you thought baseball players ought
to defect!

Otuardo asked us what we wanted to do, and

we decided to visit his godfather, who was a babalowa. We found his godfather, a large man of African descent, working behind the counter at a store catering to ration cards. Cuban citizens are given cards that allow them to receive certain items on a monthly basis. Staple items include rice, beans, sugar, coffee, eggs (14), chicken (1 pound), salt, and don't forget everybody gets one roll per day. Other items such as soap, detergent, cornmeal, crackers, and so on, are doled out on an "as needed" basis. I'm glad it's not my job to keep track of who needs and who doesn't. It looked like they all needed to me. Anyway, enough about the rations and back to the babalowa.

When there was a break in the action, the babalowa motioned Otuardo, Dusty, and I into the back room to discuss some Santeria. Along the way, we stopped to sample a little "bathtub rum", before it was placed in second-hand *Bacardi* or *Ronrico Rum* bottles for resale on the black market. We crowded into a little office where Otuardo's godfather gave us the lowdown upon the basics of Santeria. He began by taking out a string of shells from a locked box. He proceeded to explain, in Spanish, what the many combinations of the eight shells meant to one's life. For example: Two shells up and six shells down might signify prosperity and on the other hand, four shells down and four shells up could spell misfortune. He broke out a myriad of stained, ruffled papers, that described the process in great detail.

Otuardo did an admirable job of translating what we couldn't understand. We might not have understood in English either, as there was a loud generator drowning out most of what was said. The babalowa even took out his board, covered with a chalky substance that he utilized for reading futures. None of us wanted to know ours. Before leaving, I obtained a prize possession...A Che Guevara two-peso piece from the babalowa.

An Argentine by birth, Che Guevara is immortalized by Cubans as the hero of the

Revolution. His likeness is everywhere: On billboards, t-shirts, and coins. A university is named for him. We went to see his famous Cadillac in the museum...But were told it was in for repairs. I think maybe Fidel was driving Che's car around town.

A word on billboards...They're a bit different than what you might find driving down I-10 in the United States. Instead of a billboard promoting Chief Yellowhorse's trading post, you find instead, beaming portraits of Che Guevara or Fidel and Raul Castro. Advertising is unnecessary, since everything is owned by the state. Thus the billboards pay tribute to the glorious revolution or exclaim happy themes with smiling cartoon characters basking in the sunshine living life to its fullest, while doctors are busy making $21 a month. Oh, sorry...Back to happier themes.

Parched after our discussion with the babalowa, we decided to head to a cantina to have a cerveza or two. Being in Cuba, we of course wanted to sample Cuban beers. Therefore we drank Bucanero and Cristal beers. Both are very good lager-type beers and both are bottled by the same company, that being Fidel's company. They are also fuerte, or high in alcoholic content. Beers were a dollar apiece. Sounds downright reasonable until you remember what the going wage is for the average citizen. It was Otuardo's lucky day. As our guide, he was treated to mucho Bucaneros, while we were treated to many Cuban locales, many of which we would never have had the opportunity to see without him. So we treated Otuardo the best we could over the next three days. Unfortunately, we spent a little too much money in the Florida Keys and the Everglades prior to our trip, so our cash was dwindling at a fast clip. We even passed on Gator Willie's airboat ride through the everglades in an effort to save money for Cuba. Ordinarily, it's not a big deal to hit an ATM or take a cash advance out on your credit card. However, it's not only hard, but impossible to do those things in Cuba. No

American credit cards or debit cards are accepted. Once we were out of cash, we were out. And you better have enough for the exit tax, or I guess you don't leave? Maybe we would have had to move in with Otuardo until we made enough money to go home? It probably would have taken three or four weeks to wash enough dishes in order to obtain the $20 departure tax.

Feeling a bit hungry, we ventured to a paladar. But, prior to entering the paladar, we ran into an acquaintance of Otuardo's who had a line on Cuban cigars. It seemed everybody had a line on Cuban cigars. Hustlers on the street, attempted to sell foreigners rolled up crap and pass it off as the real deal. This particular fellow apparently worked for one of the government-owned factories in Havana, or a friend of his did...Just another way to make a living. It was hard to blame them.

Since we were low on funds and couldn't afford a whole box of Cohibas (which was a screaming deal at $50-60 USD), we talked the guy into selling us two for $5 a piece. He disappeared to locate the cigars and we stepped inside the paladar for some grub.

Paladares are privately run restaurants that operate throughout Cuba. There are strict restrictions placed on the paladares so that they don't steal business away from the government. Each paladar is limited to twelve seats. They can't legally serve beef, since all cattle are the property of the Cuban government. Forget about shrimp and lobster as well. These can only be *legally* consumed at state-run restaurants. That doesn't mean that there aren't paladares offering flank steaks, but you'll probably have to eat it in the back room with the limpiosos, or dishwashers. What does that leave to eat at the paladar you may ask? Pork, chicken, and fish. Served with rice and black beans. We opted for the chicken. I can't remember exactly how much the meal was, but it wasn't cheap. Otuardo was in hog heaven, as he rarely enjoys the opportunity to eat out. He snarfed down his chicken and washed it down with

a few Bucaneros. We watched the Cuban World
Series on television as we ate our meal.

As we ate, a dark beauty named Mariem walked
in and Otuardo, catching Dusty's lusty look
toward her, asked her to come over and join us.
Mariem was a 24-year old dancer (an upstanding
dancer, not a pole-spinner). She spoke very
little English and my Spanish wasn't working all
that well at the time either. Otuardo asked her
if she wanted to hang out with us for the
evening and she took off to change, arriving
back in no time with a smile on her face. Not
knowing where to head too next, we allowed
Otuardo to make the moves. He decided we should
go party underneath the great Jesus statue
across the harbor from the Morro Castle. So we
squeezed into a cab and drove through narrow,
winding roads, up a steep hill to the Jesus
statue that overlooked the twinkling lights of
Havana below. It was a beautiful sight, as a
gentle Caribbean breeze blew in off the ocean.
We ordered some Bucaneros and took in the sights
and sounds of young Cubans in their element.
Many were busy drinking rum and eating peanuts
from the vendors walking by. I tried to figure
out how they afforded their drinks? Mariem
attempted to show Dusty how to dance and if
nothing else, it was funny as hell.

After a few hours beneath Jesus, we managed
to catch a taxi back down the hillside and into
Old Havana. We dropped Mariem safely off at her
flat and then wandered around through the
darkened streets stopping every so often to
converse with someone Otuardo knew. He seemed
to know everyone.

Our next form of transport was probably the
most ridiculous rig I'd ever ridden in. Not the
most run down or primitive, but decidedly the
most ridiculous. The taxi looked more like a
toy than a taxi. It was a bright yellow,
fiberglass contraption with three wheels and a
scooter engine. Technically, and I think
legally, it was designed for two riders that sit
in the back behind the driver. Since there was
three of us I thought we should perhaps opt for

another form of transport. However, Otuardo happened to know the taxi driver and she allowed all three of us to sit behind her as we careened around corners and made our way to several establishments and watering holes. We must have looked pretty damn peculiar...That's all I can say.

Finally arriving back at our hotel, we bid Otuardo adieu for the night after he informed us that he wasn't allowed to come up to our humble room. The lobby was as far as he was allowed to go by his government. No fraternization. If you happened to meet a nice Cuban woman and wanted a nightcap in your room...Better pay off the hotel manager, or it's a no-go for sure.

The following day Otuardo took the day off from work and bummed around the city with us. We walked the ocean boardwalk around to Morro Castle; a stronghold built in the late 1500s to keep out pesky French privateers. An additional wall around the city was constructed between 1674 and 1740, which repelled the pirates, but did little to deter the British, who attacked in 1762 and eventually forced the Spanish to surrender. The British held Havana for eleven months, before handing it back to Spain in exchange for Florida.

We continued on past ruins of antiquity and modernity alike, stopping at several markets only to be accosted by illegal cigar salesmen and pushy trinket traders. We toured churches, squares, and museums, stopping occasionally to slug down a Bucanero or two.

One of the afternoon highlights was the visit to the Hotel Ambos Mundos, where Ernest Hemingway resided in room No. 511. He lived there during the 1930s, prior to purchasing an estate called Finca la Vigia on the outskirts of Havana in 1939. Hemingway lived at Finca La Vigia until 1960, when he moved to Idaho. The hotel room is a museum, complete with Hemingway's bed, typewriter and initial scrawlings of *For Whom the Bell Tolls*. The hotel has a 1930s feel to it even today. Then again, so does much of Cuba. Hemingway impersonators hung out in the lobby bar.

We retired to our hotel for the local Spanish custom of siesta, which is either a great way of living life to its fullest or just an excuse to be a lazy ass bum. We watched a little cable television and relaxed. By the way, cable television is illegal for Cuban citizens, but deemed a must for tourists.

Two hours later Otuardo and Mariem were in the lobby calling us down for some more malfeasance. We went out to a cantina in Old Havana for drinks. There was plenty going on inside the bar/restaurant, which is fairly typical for many Latin American locales. There almost always seem to be stray dogs walking the beat, looking for some scraps and this particular establishment was no exception. The place even boasted a steamy fashion show. Smiling hookers gave us the once, twice, and three times over. One young lady of the evening came over and sat down beside me, placing her hand on my knee and asking most intensely if I was planning on going to the "hotel or the house"? I of course declined, but couldn't resist asking her how much, at which point she became aggravated and stormed away. Watching the women work the tourists was entertaining as hell. I know, I know...It really is sad and despicable, but entertaining as hell nevertheless.

The next drifter to visit our table was a street kid in need of a pen. We waved him away a few times, but after several Bucaneros and a fuzzy (not teary mind you, but fuzzy no less) change of heart, I decided to give him my pen. Not just any pen, but a genuine TPAC pen, one of my dad's vintage company pens that had been in my dresser drawer since the 1980s. I'm surprised it even wrote. It was a large, shiny utensil, which the kid happily skipped away with.

At that point, Otuardo became truly saddened, telling us how he had to buy his own paper and pens and even his own "doctor coat". He couldn't get the pen off his mind. I felt

horrible and had I known he was so taken by the
pen, I would have gladly given the pen to him
instead of to the kid. Although, I would have
to say the kid was a better artist than Otuardo.
The kid returned a half-hour later with a
comical, side-view napkin portrait of Dusty and
I. Apparently, he was off to our left, outside
the bar, sketching our ugly mugs. I sure hope I
look better from the other side.

We bought dinner for Otuardo and Mariem, as
Dusty and I chose to fast and diet on Bucaneros
instead. My buddy Jason Moore used to always
tell me that beer was in fact food and I guess
I've tried to prove his thesis correct a time or
three since. Sometimes it pans out...And other
times, well...Frankly...It doesn't. In all
honesty, the food looked a bit shaky at that
particular establishment, and I could do without
the gurgles for awhile. Fireworks in the air
are really cool...Fireworks in your belly are
really shitty.

After the entertainment died down, we
decided to head back to the hotel and call it a
night. Dusty and Mariem had been hitting it off
fantastically and were eager to get to know each
other better if you catch my drift.
Unfortunately, two consenting adults wanting to
share intimacy in Old Havana isn't exactly
embraced by the authorities. It's actually
easier to have intimacy with a hooker than a
pretty Cuban girl not charging for her time.

We walked back toward the hotel and on the
way, Otuardo having a brainstorm, stopped to ask
a woman he knew if she would rent out a room for
Dusty and Mariem to get better acquainted in for
the evening. The woman had no room to spare,
but her friend around the corner did. As we
walked casually down the cobbled, beat, smelly
street, I couldn't get over the silly fact that
I was walking down the road with a woman my
mother's age who was looking into renting a room
for some carnal knowledge. Funny thing was, it
all seemed very routine to everyone but Dusty
and I.

Otuardo, Dusty and Mariem suddenly

disappeared into an apartment building and left me standing beside the initial woman (what the hell should I call her? Madam numero uno?). At this point, I can only relate what Dusty described to me...Having not been there myself.

He says they walked into an apartment occupied by a family and then a kindly Cuban woman proceeded to show him a bedroom that happened to be unoccupied for the moment. Not exactly the guest bedroom. He had misgivings to begin with and now those misgivings became screaming voices in his head. The trio retreated from the apartment and after meeting me on the street; we were on the move...Literally. Apparently an undercover agent had been spotted down the road by Otuardo and Mariem and he was fast approaching. To be honest with you, I never saw anyone, let alone an undercover agent. But, what the hell do I know, I don't live in Havana and I don't usually knock on peoples' doors and ask them if I can have sex in their not-so-spare-room.

So we were off, not quite running, but definitely speed walking in the general direction of our hotel. "Let's go, let's go", was Otuardo's theme song as we scampered through dark alleys with Mariem peeking around the corner to see if the chase was still on. If I was in Arizona, it all would have seemed surreally ridiculous. But, I wasn't, so we boogied in and around corners to the hotel at which point Otuardo bid us a quick farewell as he and Mariem kept their dance alive, quickly ducking down the next dark alleyway.

Dusty and I hurried inside the hotel and ran up the stairs to the fourth floor. We opened the balcony doors and stepped outside. Sure enough there was a guy hanging out on the corner looking from side to side in mild desperation. Dusty and I never even saw the guy until that very moment. We just laughed. Then we just prayed Otuardo wasn't in any trouble. We could just see the headlines in the newspaper: *Doctor Indicted in Sex Ring...Cattle Prod to Follow.*

The next morning we said goodbye to Otuardo

at the hotel bar. Miraculously, he was allowed in the bar...At least for awhile anyway. After a short conversation, we were off to the airport for the quick flight back to Miami. Arriving at the airport, we snapped a few pictures of the Che Guevara billboards in the parking lot. The parking lot by the way was completely empty. And I mean completely empty. Sadly, no one was leaving Havana, or at least not many, and flights are real scarce at the international terminal.

After waxing nostalgic with Che, we walked into the tiny terminal and huddled with the few fortunate people readying themselves for America. As we passed through customs, I asked the agent to stamp my passport. He just smiled and shook his head no. I shook my head affirmatively back at him and he shrugged his shoulders as if to say "are you sure"? I figured that since I had to go through all that trouble getting tickets and permission, that I should at least get a Cuban stamp in my passport for my efforts. I was legal after all. He laughed and stamped and we were both happy. Probably laughed about it over dinner.

As we passed through the x-ray machines, a tired, bored old gentleman shook his wand at us from a distance. He saved his energy for women, whom he wanded continually. Only women were wanded. If a guy happened to walk through and set off every buzzer in the place, he gave him a bored look and gestured him through with a nod of his head. After about fifteen minutes, the power went out. As the authorities attempted to rectify the problem, a man walked right through the ungenerized x-ray machine and took a seat on a bench next to us. We just laughed. Could have brought an arsenal with him...Hell, he didn't even realize he'd gone through undetected...And neither did anyone else but us. We swam easily through U.S. customs and soaked in the fierce Florida rays as we lost ourselves on the streets of Miami...Most literally. Meanwhile, Otuardo and Mariem's crazy, desperate lives lay a mere ninety long miles to the south.

Rocky Times in Puerto Penasco

Mexico, 1991

A while back, I took a trip down south of
the border to a place in Mexico called Puerto
Penasco, or Rocky Point as any gringo that's
ever been will surely tell you. It's only about
five hours from my home in Phoenix situated on
the extreme northeastern coast of the Gulf of
California. Although in Mexico, the place is
very much overrun by Arizonans on holiday. A
place to get drunk and stupid. And after all, a
friend once told me while driving around in
Rocky Point, more specifically Cholla Bay, that
"they love us down here".

It was Thanksgiving weekend and after a
round of bird or two, I met up with my old buddy
Gary Anderson, a fellow teacher and all around
good guy. We stuffed a couple of three-wheelers
in the back of his old 1977 Chevy Long bed, two-
wheel drive pickup and headed to the first
convenient store we came across for provisions.
Provisions being pretty damned light. Ice,
beer, and maybe a bag of pretzels. Like my idol
Hayduke from Edward Abbey's *The Monkey Wrench
Gang*, we measured distance by lobbing dead
soldiers into the bed of the pickup. I
know...Stupid yes...but we were young, and at
least we didn't throw them on the side of the
highway like Hayduke did!

There we were, making haste to the fabled
seaside oasis in the midst of the desert, bird
in our bellies, a cool breeze through the open
cab windows, and sunrays reflecting off the
silver cans in our hands. About an hour over
the border and an hour from our destination, we
pulled off the road to distance ourselves from

the liquids we had ingested and promptly became stuck in the sand. You see, Gary's truck ran like a champ, but it had a few things going against it...Namely bald tires and its lack of four-wheel drive capabilities. Luckily, we had the foresight to bring along a thick chain. We had actually brought it along to lock up the bikes, but it quickly served a dual purpose. The chain became our savior, getting us out of a tough spot on at least a half-dozen occasions. Thanks again to all you good people out there that pulled us out, wherever you may be.

An hour later, we arrived at a hotel several miles from the ocean at the head of a dirt road which leads to Cholla Bay and famed J.J.'s Cantina. We rented a room for the night and chained up our bikes to a post in front of the hotel. Quite a romantic image don't you think? Like the Old West itself.

We headed down the dirt track to Cholla Bay, an American haven, where the Mexicans lease land to gringos and gringos in turn build everything from flophouses to magnificent haciendas. A golf course has recently been added at Sandy Beach, officially embossing the United States seal on the locale. Had we headed the other direction from our hotel, we would have wound up in the town of Puerto Penasco, which is not touristy and altogether Mexican in nature.

My friend Jason Moore can probably tell you all about the fine history of the famed J.J.'s Cantina. Who the original owner was and currently is and so forth, but I'm afraid I can't, nor will I ever be able to. Basically, because I don't give a shit. The bar, a spring break favorite, is decked out with license plates and paraphernalia on the walls from all over the country...America that is. Satellite dishes beam down sports and sitcoms alike from Mexico's busy industrial neighbor to the north. There are plenty of cold Mexican beers and a small parquet dance floor.

The joint was jumpin' as we entered and we decided to just go with the flow. Drink and dance and do our best to impress all the fine young Mexican...Err, I mean American...Girls. About that time of evening (not anymore mind you, for Gary's a reformed, upstanding citizen these days), Gary would transform himself into a comical alter ego named Bill. I don't know why he chose the name Bill? I think his alias was intended to conceal his true identity from ugly women. The ugly designation of course changing progressively throughout the evening. His profession varied, depending on his mood, from stockbroker, to real estate agent, to architect or simply a down-home potbelly pig farmer from Taos, New Mexico. I know what you're thinking. What a low-down, dirty thing to do. But admit it, most of those singles bars are one big pile of plasticity to begin with anyway.

He even had a particular maneuver where he got down on one knee in the middle of the bar and asked women to marry him. He claims his success rate while employing the "marriage maneuver" was 5 out of 10. One particular evening at a now-defunct nightspot in North Phoenix, he employed his goofy tactic during a power outage, substituting a purse for the Holy Scripture and a lighter as the Sacred Candle. He took that one home. Silly I know!

This time however, things went wrong from the get go. He targeted a striking blonde with all her teeth and a little too much to drink across the bar. She favored his attention all right, but her behemoth of a boyfriend didn't take it to well. Especially the marriage ceremony bit.

Sipping my umpteenth Negra Modelo, I watched the whole ugly scene unfold across the small, crowded bar. The Giant and nine of his closest compadres (as it turned out a group of firefighters from Phoenix) encircled "Bill" and planned his untimely funeral in the exact spot that he was busy conducting his mock wedding proposal.

Having to do something, I hurried to the center of the circle, which was now tightly surrounding Gary and pled with the Giant for some sort of peaceful resolution. After some very intense moments and a whole lot of abusive language from the crowd, I somehow managed to get Gary out of there with the stolid promise that we would meet the Giant "at the hill" the next afternoon. Of course, I had no idea where or even what the hell "the hill" was, this being my first trip to Cholla Bay. But it sure sounded good at the time. A whole hell of a lot better than the alternative...Facing off against ten drunken guys and bleeding all the way to some seedy Mexican jail.

So, we managed to make a run for it before the Giant and his entourage changed their minds.

After unsticking Gary's stuck truck in the parking lot, we vamoosed to the hacienda for some much-needed rest. Good thing the Giant wasn't chasing us...We wouldn't have gotten very far.

The next morning we awoke to find our three-wheelers in the same spot we left them...Always a plus. We dined on huevos rancheros at the hotel restaurant and enjoyed spectacular ocean views from the second-story balcony. The ocean looked real nice, but the restaurateur's daughter looked even nicer. It was tough to decide which one to focus on.

After a fulfilling meal, we hopped on the bikes and headed down the rutted, jolting road toward Cholla Bay. We had pretty much forgotten about the averted big rumble, but kept an eye out for the Giant just in case. We were after all in our mid-twenties and not in our mid-teens.

On the way to Cholla Bay, we passed by the now infamous "hill" off to our left. More like a small desert mountain with its northern slope eroded down to sand. The sandy side of course appealing to the off-road enthusiasts which were busy racing around at top speeds, some tumbling, all of them eating dust and drinking lots of beverages despite the fact it was ten in the morning.

We toured the beach for awhile then grabbed a liquid lunch at the Pataya Bar. Afterwards, we amused ourselves by watching gringo tents pinwheel down the beach in the strong winds. A few unfortunate souls buried their small cars axle-deep in the sand while driving down the beach. I couldn't imagine where they thought they were headed?

On our way back to the hotel, we visited the hill and raced around for awhile. No Giant in sight.

After a refreshing cold shower and a bite to eat, we were ready to see the Mexican side of Mexico. This entailed a trip into the town of Puerto Penasco itself, where gringos only ventured during daylight hours. We had also heard of a fabulous house of ill repute rumored to be located in the vicinity. Now, I don't want you to think that we were down on our luck and destitute (we might have been, I don't really recall). We were far more concerned with the experience of finding the fabled whorehouse than actually taking part in any malfeasance.

In Puerto Penasco, we found a small cantina off one of the main streets and clambered in for a beer and some intel on the aforementioned sinful sight. We were the only gringos in the place and every eye was upon us as we took a seat at the bar. The mood lightened when I attempted to speak some Spanish. An intoxicated character lacking teeth, insisted we buy some shrimp. However, the way he pronounced shrimp in English sounded more like schwinn, and I couldn't stop thinking the guy wanted to sell us a bicycle. He was so persistent that the bartender had to threaten him with a baseball bat in order to leave us in peace. It was actually pretty damn comical.

We finished up our beers and procured a small clue as to the whereabouts of the whorehouse from one of the fine patrons at the bar. Then we headed out. Unfortunately the schwinn salesman followed us out to the truck, convinced we needed some seafood. He went as far as to grab a hold of Gary's door handle and block him from getting in his truck. I picked up a rock (a gesture known to traverse cultural barriers worldwide) and gently persuaded him;

letting him know that we really didn't need any shrimp. Then we got the hell out of there.

Following vague directions, we arrived at some sort of disco bar on the outskirts of Puerto Penasco. It definitely didn't resemble a whorehouse, but then again I really didn't know what did, having never actually seen one before. We were thirsty anyway, so we went in and ordered a beer and soaked in the scene. No gringos as we expected, just a lot of drinking and dancing. A couple of amigos sauntered by and we struck up a conversation, inquiring about the target one more time.

"Ssii...Ahh...Ssii..." They exclaimed. I wasn't really convinced that they knew what the hell we were talking about, but we decided to give it a try anyway. I figured at the very least they could get us Mexican rates on beer, as Americans tend to pay inflated prices in comparison. The four of us piled into Gary's truck and bounced east down a dirt track in the desert, driving ever further away from Puerto Penasco and miles away from the hotel and Cholla Bay. After about ten minutes, we arrived at what looked like a huge warehouse in the middle of nowhere. Being young and stupid, we quickly set aside our apprehensiveness and went inside. The place was cavernous and virtually empty, and it more resembled a supermarket that recently went belly-up than a bar. There were several tables and a long wooden bar occupied by a few drunks.

We grabbed a table and ordered a round of tequila from the waitress. A short while later, two obese senoritas in their early fifties appeared from the back and sashayed over to our table. They proceeded to make themselves at home by sitting down next to Gary and I. Our tour-guiding Mexican compadres gave us a wink of satisfaction. Gary and I just looked at each other and began laughing. The senoritas however, weren't impressed, and their faces had an air of complete seriousness.

I guess this was Puerto Penasco's version of the Mustang Ranch. After several drinks and much haggling, we managed to somehow escape the senorita's wrath and get the hell out of there before we were forced to commit some sort of heinous act.

The amigos assured us they knew of "otro" (other for you gringos) places for us to see and we headed farther out into the desert. At that point, we just wanted to drop these guys off and make a hasty retreat back to the hotel. After convincing our new found friends of that fact, we started heading back toward the distant lights of Puerto Penasco. And I do mean distant lights. After a mile or so, we all decided a pit stop was in order to relieve ourselves. There we were, in lovely Old Mexico, moon beaming down on us and a cool, gentle breeze blowing in off the ocean...Drunk and happy.

But suddenly one of the Mexicans jumped into the driver's seat of Gary's running truck and prepared to make off with it, leaving us stranded in the desert. His buddy wasn't impressed, as he watched with wide eyes on the other side of me, waiting to see the outcome.

Like a strange scene unfolding out of a *Starsky and Hutch* episode, the thief let out the clutch and slowly began to drive away. Instinctively, Gary ran alongside and leaped into the bed. From there, he quickly made his way up to the driver's side window, where he reached inside and grabbed the guy around the neck, simultaneously pinning his head to the rear window of the cab. The truck came to a herky-jerky stop and Gary, in complete disbelief, angrily flung the outcast hombre out of the truck and into a heap in the dirt. His friend, looking almost pale under the moon's rays, gave me a nervous look as if to say: *I had no idea he was going to do that*. Gary gave the thief a tongue-lashing and we jumped in the cab and peeled out, leaving them behind. Somehow, we managed to make our way back to the hotel. *(Editor's disclaimer: I don't personally condone any of these actions. But at the time, it sure was a hell of a lot of fun.)*

The Legendary Jim Fitzgerald

Alaska, 1997

While camped near the town of Hope, Alaska, my friend Dusty Decarlo and I happened upon a man named Jim Fitzgerald. Definitely not a famous man by any stretch, but an authentic man just the same. Alaska conjures up images of grizzly bears, wolves, glaciers, sled teams, wide-open spaces and courageous individuals battling the fierce elements. To be sure, those things and much, much more exist in Alaska. But let us not forget about the many tortured souls who migrate to Alaska in order to escape society and in extreme cases...Reality. Jim falls somewhere in that continuum.

We were contemplating camping in an abandoned (closed for the winter) campground near a creek. When I say contemplating, we were sitting on a picnic table deciding if we should sleep in the cab of the truck, seats reclined, as we had become quite accustomed to, or if we should actually set up a tent...A proper camp. The capsule idea won out, as it did on many a night during the 37-day, 10,000-mile odyssey from Cleveland, Ohio to Alaska and back. Fact was, we wouldn't have been in the campground at all if we had to pay. We made a pact in the beginning of the trip that we would pay for neither a hotel room nor a campground space on the entire journey. Which by the way, we succeeded in doing. We ended up with a little extra cash in our pockets and a little extra crust on our bodies due to our every-fifth-day-shower schedule.

Back to the tale. Like I said we were sitting on this picnic table in southern Alaska, which resembles Ireland in a way, with low-growing vegetation, sparse trees, green grass and an outwardly emerald appearance. Adjacent to the little campsite, ran a small creek. Which is pretty ironic, since there isn't much about Alaska, which is little. The creek attracted the aforementioned figure, Jim Fitzgerald. He was merely attending to his daily chores. We really didn't think much of it when he pulled hastily into the parking lot in his battered 1973 Chevrolet truck. Nor when he emerged in tattered clothing, minus the elbows, carrying pots and pans toward the creek. He grunted a greeting and walked into the creek, not to the bank, but directly in (remember it was pretty cold out). In the midst of his dish cleaning, he proceeded to warn us about the terrible itch a man can contract from the creek. "You guys better stay clear of this creek, it gives a man a powerful itch", he yelled over to us as he stood knee deep in the middle of the current. Maybe he was immune? From that time forward, we've always referred to any itch that we incurred as the "Jimmy Itch".

After finishing up his chores, Jim flopped down belly first on top of his truck hood and conversed with us for awhile. Jim said that he'd been living in a fifth wheel around the bend a ways for the past several months. "It's not like I'm homeless or anything; I just don't have anywhere else to go". Damn Forest Service is kicking me out soon though", he stated.

He told us that he had some sort of a mining claim that he shared with his "big brother", who was coming back sometime soon to pick him up. We were never quite able to ascertain from what he told us if this "big brother" character, was in fact his real big brother, a friend, or a figment of his imagination? He told us that Wednesday mornings were his favorite...The day a ranger named Donna came by to clean the commodes. "Damn fine looking woman that one, even if she is cleaning shitters for a living".

After shooting the breeze with Jim upon the finer points of National Forest living, he retreated back up to his homestead, inviting us up "later on".

After eating dinner (probably a can of beans or some similar generic fare), I loaded up my shotgun (always that threat of a hungry bear or a really stupid grouse) and we hoofed it up to Jim's camp.

His trailer was nestled among some trees, partially hidden from view, about three hundred yards upstream from Six-Mile Creek. We no sooner came within proximity of the door, when it jerked wide open and a grizzled hand extended outward for a shake. "How you boys doin', my name's Jim Fitzgerald" (Although I've been calling him by name this entire time, in truth we never dispensed with formal pleasantries until this point).

After introductions, we entered the trailer and I placed my pump shotgun next to Jim's Bear rifle near the door. Great place Alaska, where it's just commonplace to carry around firearms. Might have been lighter to carry around a handgun, but the Canucks don't savvy Yanks transporting them across their borders.

Jim showed us into his modest trailer and directed us to sit down at the table, where he must have spent countless, lonely hours peering out the windows at the beautiful scenery surrounding him. He could have passed for 70, although he was only in his early fifties. He donned an old blue and gray flannel shirt minus the aforementioned elbows. His affable blue eyes were surrounded by a snowy head of hair and a white beard that extended all the way down his throat like a gizzard.

He wore glasses, but mainly preferred to peer over them at you instead of through them. Jim proceeded to give us a lecture upon the importance of keeping one's feet dry. Always a good rule to follow no doubt, especially in Alaska. The odd thing was, he espoused these ideals to us while attired in soaking wet socks and tennis shoes, as we sat there in dry boots and socks. Faint images of *To Build a Fire* rummaged vaguely through my mind.

We asked Jim if he wanted a cigar, which he gladly accepted, stating "hell yes I smoke, like to smoke cocaine too, but that's another story altogether". Jim possessed quite a hack, and we wondered if he might have been suffering from tuberculosis? Jim recounted his life, stating that he was a Vietnam vet, who had broken his neck twenty years prior by diving headlong into a shallow lake, where he landed ungracefully on a brick. He hadn't worked since "on account of the pain". Ironically, he found little difficulty living alone in the wilds of Alaska. Jim said he had "pickled his brain" throughout years of binge drinking and heavy alcohol abuse.

He was however, a remarkable aviation historian, recounting a horde of specifics and interesting stories. He even possessed a small library on the topic. Jim said he needed to "head back to the valley (Anchorage) before the snow flew". He was just waiting for his "big brother" to come and pick him up. He never did call this person by name. Just seemed wacky to me that he kept calling him his big brother, something a kid might have said, not a fifty-year old adult?

Jim offered us some burned, raw-in-the-middle, fluffy, volcano-shaped biscuits, that we graciously declined, having just eaten and all. He said it was the first time the stove in his trailer had ever been fired up. We wondered what the hell he'd been eating for the past three months? He asked us if we desired the lights around the table turned on and we said it didn't matter. He then proceeded to turn them all on...For about two, silent, tense, nerve-racking minutes. He then quickly turned them off and told us how he jumped the trailer battery with his truck battery and vice-a-versa. And what a pain in the ass it was.

He then broke into a tale about a couple of "German or Swiss guys that had broke down and fucked his gas situation all to hell". Apparently these guys had broken down and required a ride into the town of Hope for a part some eight miles away. Jim railed on them for a good ten minutes. Telling us over and over how they disrupted his fragile budget.

He then relayed a story about a friend that had recently been evicted from his apartment in Anchorage. He said that his friend's landlady had clearly discriminated against him based on his color. "My friend, he's a spade, but he's a pretty decent guy." The bitch said he was sellin' crack, which he was, but what the hell; she didn't know that, the whole affair was utter bullshit", exclaimed Jim.

Soon thereafter, we felt we had stayed our limit. Knowing something about the realm of hermitness myself, we bid Jim farewell. I don't know how long, nor if Jim is still alive, as his health was poor, but I wish him well just the same. Just another character that didn't quite seem to fit into the niche of modern Americana...Whatever that may.

Three Gringos in Peru

Peru, 2000

It took a little convincing and some future promises to visit other countries in exchange, to convince my friends Dusty Decarlo and Christian Bates to travel to Peru in search of Inca ruins and adventure. All we ever heard was how bad things were there.

Flying out of Phoenix Sky Harbor Airport, we caught another jet in Houston and then settled in for the 6 1/2-hour flight to Lima. Houston was uneventful, aside from a serenading rib cook and a female security guard that scrutinized Christian's backpack, exclaiming "who bag?", in a somewhat familiar...Detroitian language.

As we reached our seats on the plane from Houston to Lima, Dusty, who is customarily passive in such situations, ripped into a woman he assumed had wrongly captured his window seat. He attempted to speak broken Spanglish and to utilize fancy hand signals. What he didn't realize until moments later was that the woman, who was Peruvian-born and resembled an Incan woman in every way, was in fact from Tampa and spoke perfect English. And by the way, she also held a ticket that entitled her to the window seat.

Although the flight began a little uncomfortably, we were soon discussing Peru and Helen took a liking to us. She even disappeared into the banos for what seemed like half an hour to freshen up. She looked like a totally different person when she reappeared as we touched down at 10:30 p.m. in Lima. I have to admit the half-hour really did her right. She was met at the airport by no less than twenty-five Peruvian family members. We were met at the airport by no less than twenty-five Peruvian cab drivers and hotel agents.

We all enjoyed green lights at the intersection (a system that is designed to randomly stop passengers for searches) and thus avoided a search and seizure opportunity, although we really had nothing to seize anyway. You would have to be a complete idiot to bring drugs into Peru anyway, wouldn't you? Kind of akin to bringing candy to a candy store. I have often wondered if the traffic-light-type search instruments were rigged? Are they truly random? Or are there perhaps hidden buttons on the ground that are depressed by customs agents when they see somebody that appears worthy of a search? We donned our overstuffed backpacks and resembling lumbering, oversized turtles, we pushed through the madding crowd at curbside and climbed upstairs to an airport bar to await our 5:45 a.m. flight.

We enjoyed Cristal and Cuzquena beer and were entertained by watching confused travelers traverse the intersection of red and green lights below in immigration.

We eventually attempted to sleep along a wall on the second story of the airport with dozens of other grogans (a.k.a. smelly cheap bastards like us) who were avoiding hotel charges and departing early for destinations unknown. A determined floor waxer creatively gyrated between and among the many comatose bodies and unwary heads (Christian's included) to get her sheen across.

We had to stand in line for two hours prior to our actual departure time in order to obtain boarding passes. A Peruvian custom, one which is customary whether the plane is actually on time or not and oftentimes it's not. And it wasn't.

The flight began with a bang as the pilot's door flew open upon takeoff and rattled the drink cart containing the *Inca Kola* and *Fanta*. The jet was a vintage 1970s model 727, probably a hand-me-down from the United States or perhaps

Mexico? We made our landing in Cuzco...Just barely anyway...As we bounced up and down on the runway, passengers cheering wildly (a common occurrence in Latin countries). I was told afterward by the pilot that the approach is "tricky" and every safe landing is greatly appreciated. That made me feel relieved.

We had reservations at the Colonial Palace Inn, so we procured a taxi, which is almost instantaneous throughout Peru. You just have to be prepared to bargain for the price of the ride. The Nuevo Sol or monetary unit of Peru was roughly 3-1 to our exalted greenback at the time, so a cab ride of five soles ($2.67) was pretty damn cheap. The cab driver took us to the *wrong* Colonial Palace, as there were two, but soon rectified the matter and we arrived safely within the hotel lobby at 8:30 a.m. After checking in, we managed to sleep for a few hours.

We awoke lightheaded and groggy in the city of 11,000 feet. After gathering our wits and drinking some coca de mate, we strolled uptown to the Plaza de Armas (The center of just about every Spanish-designed city). The streets were cobbled and covered in an oily sheen, a sheen that becomes dangerously slippery when it rains. The streets are full of maniacal cab drivers and smog-emitting hulks. There is little method to the madness, a free-for-all of horns and brakes.

We located a fancy Incan restaurant and I sampled the filet mignon while Dusty and Christian tried the trout. I think the steak might have been alpaca or llama, but I'm not sure? It was a bit tough.

I have to sneak in a word about showers and banos. For the most part you can expect cold showers. Sometimes a lukewarm one, but seldom ever a hot one. Simply because you take the first of three, by no means guarantees you a hot one. Sometimes quite the opposite. The actual showering facilities themselves weren't bad at all in Peru, just the temperature itself. We even had the distinct displeasure of a shower in Puno that scorched our skin. It seemed to lack any cold water, just scathing hot. A lot of hotels in Peru turn their water off at night, so if you have the unfortunate occasion to unleash an angry bowel movement in the dark of night, it might stick with you until morning. Unless of course you got real lucky and it all went down on the first flush. Toilets for the most part were excellent. I don't know about a system whereby you throw your used paper in a garbage can next to the toilet, which was the case in most establishments, but we didn't have to battle the toilets for the most part.

On Saturday, we strolled uptown and bought a horseback ride for 15 Soles/$5 USD. We followed a caballero up the hills of Cuzco to the ruins of Sacsayhuaman about a thousand feet above the city and the site of his rancherita. We bought a "tourist card" for $5 thanks to Dusty, who acting quick on his feet, produced an Arizona driver's license that entitled us to the student rate. Since the guy selling us the pass had no idea what he was looking at, he accepted it as student identification. So, we saved $5, which paid for the horseback ride.

The horses were tired, old vagabonds that unfortunately have seen to many ruins and not enough hay. But what the hell, for $5, one can't complain. The four-hour horseback ride took us to Qenko, The Temple of the Moon, Puca Pucara, Tambo Machay and back to Sacsayhuaman.

Qenko, which literally means "labyrinth" was the site of many rituals and was complete with both a sacrificial table and an altar to go along with the many intricate carvings. The main themes of the carvings in Incan, and for many other pre-Incan peoples as well, are the Condor, Puma and the Snake. The Condor represents the heavens and the future. The Puma represents the earth and mortal existence. The Snake represents death, the past, and the bowels of the earth. Canals carved into the rock at Qenko, enabled the Inca priests to pour chicha, (a distilled corn brew) mixed with llama's blood into the cracks. The outcome or path that the liquids took determined the fate of the tribe.

Either good or bad. There are also rocks that outlined certain animals. The images appeared on the solstices and also when the sun shone through on certain dates. It was all quite bizarre. The largest image is an 18-foot high Puma which resides within an ancient amphitheater.

We had to watch our footing around the various ruins as *Big Brother* was far away in the States along with his warning signs, waivers, and disclaimers. There was no one to sue if you fell off of the rocks and broke your silly neck. A rather refreshing thought. Too many damn victims in the United States. All wanting their own form of retribution and justice. One thing a visitor from the United States notices right away is the freedom he has to roam around the ruins. Of course on the flipside, this can also become a double-edged sword if someone abuses the privilege and destroys the artifacts.

Qenko was a ceremonial center dedicated to the worship of the sun (Pacha Mama). Unlike Sacsayhuaman, which was created by moving monstrous rocks, Qenko was carved out of a gigantic slab of limestone; complete with a subterranean room formerly utilized for sacrifice.

The Temple of the Moon was off the bus circuit (horses only) and out in the sticks so to speak. We passed a pack of wild dogs and rode through a climate dominated by the sun. If the clouds obscured it, it was cold. If the sun shone through, it was hot. Not much in between.

High Andean foothills rose on either side of us. Beautiful, lonely looking, 20,000-foot peaks covered in ice, dotted the horizon. The temple itself held more sacrificial tables and a passageway through the mountain, which once was a shortcut for messengers who traveled back and forth between the various centers of importance. There were also multiple caves and crude living quarters.

Passing carefree llamas and ever-present dog societies, we moved on to Puca Pucara, a fortress, which most likely guarded the road to the Sacred Valley. The complex features towers, stairways, and tunnels that overlook hillside terraces. I gave a few peanuts to an indigent dog that resembled the *Taco Bell* Dog. Yo Quiero...Peanuts!

By this time our male anatomies were suffering quite horribly. It would have helped if we were better horseback riders. The horses tried to knock us off a few times and Dusty's saddle almost fell off completely, but other than that, it was an awesome experience.

We parked our ponies near the road and walked a ways up a dirt road to Tambo Machay, the sacred bathing place for Inca rulers and their royal beauties. Miraculously, water still flows down through a series of aqueducts, which once fed life to various water rituals. It was hard to comprehend that the ancient aqueducts remained operative, withstanding severe earthquakes and the test of time.

Last, but much more than least, we investigated Sacsayhuaman, which was the last stronghold of Manco Inca in his attempt to hold Cuzco, the Incan Capital and thwart the attacks of the Spanish Conquistadors in 1536. The complex is complete with a double wall said to resemble the teeth of a Puma, with the fort itself resembling the head. The fort boasted enough room to garrison over 5,000 soldiers and at least three towers overlooked the fields below. The rocks are unbelievably large. An incredible feat of engineering, as the space in between them is virtually nonexistent (A piece of paper won't even fit between the slabs).

The construction of the structures is even more impressive when you take into account the fact that the Inca lacked the invention of the wheel or large animals. Cuzco's water supply also begins at the fort as it runs beneath the ground through a series of stone conduits. The Inca laid siege to the Spanish in Cuzco for a period of ten months, but were ultimately unsuccessful. Historians say that the Inca may have saved their civilization if they would have won out. I don't think so, just too many damn

Spaniards waiting to come over in the name of God, Gold, or Fame...In no particular order. Francisco Pizarro, the Spanish Leader, desired so much gold, that Atuallpa, the Incan leader, inquired if his people perhaps ate the glittering stuff.

We walked back down to Cuzco in the late afternoon. Along the way I snapped a picture of an old Incan woman walking her llama up the trail. She became irate when I failed to pay her and screamed obscenities at me, or at least I think they were obscenities, not understanding Quechan, the traditional Incan language.

We discovered a restaurant overlooking the Plaza and dined on pizza (a main staple for us) and cervezas (the mainest of the main staples). Afterwards, we strolled back down the hill to our hotel and washed the horse smell off as best we could in the cool Cuzco shower water.

Later on that night we drank beer at the Cross Keys Pub, a British bar owned by archeologist and explorer, Barry Walker. Walker spends a lot of time searching for ruins and artifacts. Peru is definitely a country that allows one's *Indian Jones* imagination to run wild. There are many sites and artifacts just waiting to be discovered.

While at the bar, we met back up with two girls named Kara and Michelle, who were on the plane with us from Houston. They hailed from Lakewood, Ohio. We also met a guy named Carlos from Lima. He was a light-skinned Peruvian and during our conversation, exclaimed "my blood has never been tainted by Indian blood". There are three main ethnicities in Peru. Spaniards like Carlos, making up the minority, traditional Incan peoples, very short and stout, and mestizo (mixture) people that are a blend of the two. The Peruvian women have a very attractive look. I'm sorry I can't say the same for the men.

We hung out there for a while, then went to a crazy techno bar called Xcess with Carlos. The place was loud, smoky and happening.

Sunday morning we strolled up to Mama Afrika's on the Plaza and ate pizza again, while watching France beat Denmark in the first round of Euro 2000. The cook had a hell of a time getting the fire lit in the oven and eventually resorted to breaking up a chair from the dining room, which he fed to the fiery gods. It was the best pizza we had on the trip. Perhaps some of the other establishments ought to resort to burning their chairs as well.

Food consumption was pretty much always on our minds. What we could eat and what we couldn't. Fruit definitely must be peeled and salads for the most part, were too risky. Water from the bottle only. We had quite a few one-meal days. Feast and famine. After the pizza, we bummed around town for deals on trinkets. Spreading our limited wealth among the people of Peru as best we could.

In the evening, we dined at a fancy restaurant on the square. I tried another steak, perro (dog) perhaps?, while Dusty and Christian sampled some more trout. We also sampled the national whiskey drink, Pisco Sour, which is a brandy with egg whites and cinnamon. I didn't care that much for it. We all regretted not sampling the cuy, or guinea pig.

The waiter dissuaded us, but I really wished we had tried it anyway. It is a Peruvian delicacy and is by Peruvian standards (and to low budget travelers like us) expensive. It was 38 soles or about $13. Some restaurants had cages, similar to a lobster tank, where you could actually select your own furry critter.

Monday morning, we caught a cab to the train station and boarded a local train for Machu Picchu. We came close to running several people over on the way, as they refused to get out of the road and our cabbie wasn't about to stop. The proprietors of the tour group we booked the tickets through for the Machu Picchu tour would only release the tickets from each leg of the trip as we approached each subsequent leg. Thus the train and bus tickets were dispersed only as we boarded. Kind of strange, but what the hell, the whole damn country is a bit strange! But very loveable at the same time.

The seats in the train were made for dwarfs or Lilliputians...Take your pick. You have to actually weave knees with the opposing passenger in order to fit. The one consolation had to be the dizzying views of snow-capped Andean peaks looming right above the train. Truly awesome.

The train was slow as hell and made stops at cow pastures all over the countryside, allowing plenty of time to meet your fellow travelers. I sat with a guy from Panama named Hector, who pilots ships through the 52-mile long Panama Canal. He says it takes approximately 12 hours to negotiate the locks, while the drive back to Panama City is only about 2 hours. He works every other day for six weeks straight, then receives four weeks off. The other guy, named Oscar, was a 23-year-old from San Salvador, El Salvador. He works for Delta and is forever remembered for showing us a great chicken joint on the Plaza de Armas in Cuzco later on that night.

After a 5-hour combination of cab, train, and bus rides we pulled up to Machu Picchu. The skies were relatively clear at 8,000 feet and we could see high peaks surrounding the site for a brief while, until clouds prevailed once more and obscured our view. Machu Picchu was indeed a beautiful, magical sight to behold. I can understand how the jungle could hide it, as the growth is very thick in the vicinity. Lush, green hillsides and mountains serve to make travel around the area painstaking at best. The ruins themselves were less impressive to us than we had imagined. Don't get me wrong they were still really cool; but the stones are smaller and not quite as intricate as similar ruins around Cuzco. Workers were busy remodeling the place and that kind of bothered me, as they don't even really know what it looked like to begin with. I wondered what happened to the original rocks? Lots of questions, few answers.

We ditched the tour guide and roamed free. Probably missed a few things by doing so, but the tour thing just sucked. We hiked up and around the mountains overlooking the ruins

opposite Huayna Picchu (the prominent mountain
in most pictures of Machu Picchu), which we
weren't allowed to hike because we got there
after 1:00 p.m. We ate some coca leaves that we
bought for 1 Sole (.33 USD) on the train and
walked around the backside of Machu Picchu,
where we feasted our eyes on the continuous
whitewater churning below in the Urubamba River.

We walked as far as we could, to a bridge
that was long forgotten and decaying. We turned
around. Ironically, this bridge is pictured in
a video I show to my high school students when I
teach them about Peru. However, they must have
doctored it up a bit for the documentary. It
didn't look nearly as stable in our eyes, as it
does on the video.

We caught the train at Agua Calientes, which
is pretty much a ravenous dump, filled with
trash and poor campesinos. And of course dogs.
There are so many damned dogs in Peru that it's
not funny. Of course, I suppose that means that
there are very few cats as well. I can only
remember seeing two people actually walking
dogs...A large German Shepherd and a little kid
on the Avenue Del Sol in Cuzco, who had a puppy
with a plastic bag on its head. He was playing
a little guitar and entertaining everyone who
passed by. Other than those two, it appeared
Peruvian dogs were pretty much on their own. We
paid the five-year-old kid in Cuzco a Sole for a
Zapruder shot. We call our underhanded, bum,
and miscellaneous snapshots Zapruder shots.

Upon our return to Cuzco, Oscar led us to a
chicken shack. A half-chicken and fries for $5.
You can't beat it, especially after fasting all
day long. A word about Peruvian potatoes.
There are as many as 200 different varieties in
the Andes and the potato began its illustrious
career right here in South America. The Indians
of South America were enjoying fries much
earlier than the French ever thought about
frying them.

On Tuesday morning we awoke early and waited
impatiently for our cab to bring us to the bus
station for our $10, 7-hour ride down south to

Puno and Lake Titicaca. We watched the movie *Mafia* and wondered how many of our fellow travelers really understood the jokes...It surely couldn't have been too many. The bus driver stopped abruptly in the middle of the road at one point to have it out with a truck driver. They swore and threatened, but alas nothing came of it. No blood on the highway. No rolling around in the dirt.

On we drove, through rolling green countryside and the weekly wash being done in the rivers. We ambled slowly past adobe abodes without chimneys. Where do they cook I wondered? Very few of the homes, hotels, or buildings have heat here in the Andes. Amazing when you consider it's chilly just about every night of the year?

Puno lacks beauty. Lake Titicaca isn't all that impressive from Puno's vantage point either. There was about one strip in the city that was agreeable and the remainder that we had the misfortune to view, was grubby as hell.

The hotel agents attempting to lure us in, were on us as soon we descended the bus stairs and Christian was inadvertently separated from a guy from Colorado that he had been talking to on the ride down from Cuzco. He was fired up mad at the hoteleers, screaming at them to leave him the !$#@ alone.

We stayed at a crummy hotel without heat, which goes without saying, and a boiling hot shower. It was curiously, however, equipped with HBO and Cinemax. We dined on more chicken and I checked out the Diamondbacks progress at an internet café, as there was hardly a place in Peru where you couldn't find the net, kind of bizarre when you looked out at the meager surroundings. Christian and Dusty enjoyed some authentic Peruvian coffee (Instant Nescafe).

The bus to Bolivia picked us up Wednesday morning at our doorstep and off we went. It took three hours and we were in downtown Copacabana, Bolivia on the shores of Lake Titicaca. In contrast to Puno, the lake was beautiful here in Copacabana. Sparkling blue, crystal clear, and cold. We exchanged some Soles and discovered the Boliviano was actually 6-1 USD. We booked a room at the Del Sol, which boasted the fanciest digs in town. And since Christian paid with his credit card and we paid him back in Bolivianos, he soon became the King of Copacabana. Spreading his wealth at every store and bungalow in town. He won't admit it, shopping being sort of a fem thing and all, but he was having a hell of a good time. Damn near bought out the town. Dusty managed to procure a Che Guevara shirt...The last one in town.

A word on money and currency in South America. Don't bring or receive any ripped or torn bills. They totally abhor them. And I mean the slightest tear. Sort of ironic, since the condition of their own money pretty much sucks. U.S. change is also worthless as nobody will change it or accept it. I gave mine to various bums as a keepsake. In return, they gave me a crazed look of wonder...Or maybe that was contempt?

We decided to take a trip on a slow boat to the Island of the Sun. We sat on top and took in the 20,000-foot peaks surrounding us. The lake's elevation is around 13,000 feet and it's the highest navigable lake in the world. I had to laugh when I caught sight of a guy reading the book *Alive*. Here we were in the middle of Lake Titicaca, on this beat vessel in the Andes, and he's reading about a plane crash in the Andes where the survivors were forced to eat the dead victims' flesh. Pretty macabre stuff.

After making it to the island, we climbed up the hillside, our lungs hurting, to witness a traditional Incan festival in the little square. We had to be careful not to cut our elbows on the pieces of glass, which were placed haphazardly on top of the wall encircling the square as we watched the ceremony. A custom in Peru. Glass covered Peruvian rooftops taking their place beside bull statuettes.

We decided to sit inside the launch on the excruciatingly slow return ride back to Copacabana. It was just way too frigid outside

in the late afternoon breeze. We were horrified
to find four tiny posts supporting the upstairs
deck where we had been riding on the way to the
island. Definitely wouldn't fly in the States.
However, it was definitely par for the course in
Peru and Bolivia, where an extension ladder
simply consisted of two ladders tied together
with string.

After returning to Copacabana, we rushed to
get dinner as things shut down early in the
sleepy little town. Contrary to popular
disbelief, Peruvians don't load up on tamales,
tacos, and burritos. Those delicacies are only
available at Mexican restaurants in Peru.
Peruvians eat a lot of potatoes, peppers, corn,
trout, beef, chicken and an occasional alpaca or
llama. Maybe even an occasional dog?
Definitely an abundant supply around. As for
me, I tend to stick with pizza and chicken...In
case you hadn't noticed.

Copacabana is a low-key, romantic sort of
place. No horns blaring and no exhaust or pushy
vendors. No beggars either. Too bad I was with
two smelly dudes and not a pretty senorita, but
that's life isn't it. We all slept well. I
happily awoke throughout the night, catching
beautiful glimpses of the full moon reflecting
on the placid lake outside our window.
Spectacular beyond words...I was really
awestruck.

Thursday morning we got our showers in while
the hot water was on (7:15 a.m. -10:30 a.m.).
Then we ate as many oranges, tangerines and
apples as we could muster at the hotel
restaurant, fearing scurvy was right around the
corner.

Afterward, we headed back into town and the
"King" continued his buying spree, which he
commenced by purchasing a thatched picnic basket
to carry his wares in. We were scheduled to
catch a bus at 1:30 p.m. Bolivian time (12:30
p.m. Peruvian time) so we placed our packs in
the luggage stow and left several belongings on
the seat.

It seems the unscrupulous driver had also

booked half the bus with a Dutch tour group and agreed to leave at 3:00 p.m., while assuring us, and the rest of the bus passengers that we would leave earlier. Fortunately, Christian had noticed the bus number.

As we were relaxing in the town square above the bus station, we happened to notice the bus taking a lap around the city, preparing to leave with our bags in tow. We leaped to our feet and ran over to the bus, jumping aboard in anger and relief. We left town with all the Dutch people's bags on board. We couldn't believe that the driver could do such a thing.

We drove about twenty minutes to the border, where we disembarked to have our passports stamped. Suddenly, the bus driver turned around and went back to pick up the Dutch group, leaving us stranded for two hours in the "no man's land" between Peru and Bolivia, not technically in either country.

We were entertained by a couple of young children aged 5 and 7, who were attempting to sell postcards from Australia. With no takers, they just hung out and talked to us. We told them we had kangaroos, manatees, and koala bears in our backyards at home and that we ate them as well. They were very impressed. After a long discussion, I gave the two boys a sole each and the smile radiating from their faces will remain etched in my mind forever. The littlest kid flung his arms around me and hugged me, then disappeared beneath a wooden fence. I felt like I was watching a *Little Rascals* episode.

Upon arriving in Puno we immediately sought out a bus to Cuzco, as we had seen enough of Puno already. We met a British couple, Stuart and Elizabeth, and they asked if they could tag along with us, as they were headed to Cuzco as well. We backpacked through the grubby, crowded, narrow streets of Puno in search of Imexso's bus office. I managed to break a flowerpot, as I clumsily rambled through a tourist office with my pack dangling wildly from my back. The shopkeepers laughed and jokingly told me I owed them ten soles. I kept walking.

We found the bus terminal, booked a reservation, then hit a restaurant, where I ate fettuccine of all things and listened to traditional music. It went right through me and I had to improvise in the banos, which had no seat and no flusher. The stall next to mine possessed merely a hole in the floor (Morocco-style). I did what I could, then had to pour jugs of water down the old boy to flush away the sod. Sorry, but you can't have the romance without the cruel reality of travel.

The bus ride was long and I was seated next to an old, smelly, one-toothed Incan gentleman for six hours. He did enjoy the flick however, as he exclaimed "La pelicula es bueno". *US Marshals* was the flick...It was played in English with Spanish subtitles.

We followed a different route than we had a few days prior, this time winding through the Andean foothills down dirt roads, getting stuck momentarily in washes on more than one occasion.

We finally made it to Cuzco around 3:00 a.m. Surprisingly enough, there were plenty of hotel agents and cab drivers waiting at the bus station. They immediately swarmed us and made their pitches. Christian tired and in no mood, gave them a tongue-lashing and sent them scurrying. We ended up taking a cab to our former hotel, the Colonial Palace Inn, where we crashed hard.

We woke up late the next morning and walked uptown to do some shopping. Along the way, we stopped briefly to hand out our uneaten bus meals to less fortunate people of the streets. One guy fishing in a dumpster...Received two...His lucky day! We cashed some traveler's checks at the rate of 3.42 to 1 USD at a cambio exchange then ate broasted chicken for 7.50 Soles ($2.50). We bought a bunch of trinkets and wandered around downtown the remainder of the day.

Friday night, we met up with Stuart and Elizabeth at Los Perros, a British owned place with couches, coffee tables and board games. Although the place was pretty damned modern, I still noticed people throwing their toilet paper in the trash rather than flushing it down, something I always have a hard time fathoming.

We ate baguettes and potato skins with mayo and avocado with no problem whatsoever. We washed the delight down with a few Cristal beers. Safe food is always so appetizing when you're hungry and afraid you may get sick. After eating, we retreated to Stuart and Elizabeth's hostel up the street. where we talked and partied until two a.m. or so.

The walk home was a bit shady, as we started to walk the wrong way and were informed by *Fat Pete*, a drunk old individual, that we were headed toward muy peligroso (danger) if we kept heading in that direction. After convincing Christian we were going in the wrong direction, we skirted by the main square and passed flocks of Cuzconians pissing quietly in the night upon the ancient walls of the city.

Saturday morning, Christian and I walked up town and boarded a van that delivered us through the Sacred Valley to the Urubamba for a kayaking trip. The trip to the river was relaxing as we bullshitted with a woman from Annapolis, a professor from Ohio University, two Argentineans, a Spanish teacher and her Salvadorian man from Austin and our guides, one a crazy chick from Holland. We had to help the guide with some translation at the put-in and soon discovered we had more experience than the guide. We weren't able to figure out if he was just letting the rookies run into the rocks in the middle of the river, or if he was truly incompetent. It's always dangerous to broadside boulders...You may just end up getting wet.

The water was icy cold and the clouds above didn't help matters. The landscape was awesome despite the garbage strewn on the banks. There were only a few rapids of consequence and it wasn't very challenging for Christian who had his eye on the class V stuff downstream. I found several of the class III-IV rapids challenging enough however, especially when the guide kept insisting we follow his raft down the

rapid. To our chagrin, I might add. A kayak
moves much quicker than a raft and without
scouting or knowing anything about the river we
found ourselves right on the raft's ass and
worried about going beneath it in several of the
rapids. I walked the last rapid, which looked
like a quagmire of rocks. Christian hit the
ten-foot drop and got vertical before
cartwheeling off a rock, and over, rolling back
up, none the worse for the wear. I paddled a
Savage Gravity and Christian a Dagger RPM.
After the run, we ate fried rice, tomatoes,
cucumbers, onions and rolls. Mate de Coca tea
was also available. It felt nice to eat safe
fruit and vegetables.

We hung out with Stuart and Elizabeth again
on Saturday night and then went shopping for the
sexually explicit, comical-as-hell, Moche
people, which are curious little key chains and
ornaments in compromising positions made out of
adobe. The Moche reigned prior to the Inca and
resided on the coast, where their descendants
still ply the ocean waters in reed boats.

Sunday morning we jetted off to Lima.
Miraculously, the pilot's door flew open again
upon takeoff (it was even a different jet). The
crew distributed chocolate cigars to all of the
men for Father's Day. While waiting for our
bags in Lima, we ran into Kara Minnic from
Lakewood again. She had placed her ticket in
the front pocket of the plane and had forgotten
it on her trip to Puerto Maldonado and the rain
forest.

Since you don't need identification to use a
ticket in Peru, someone kept it and she was out
of luck. She bought a ticket straight through
to Lima and her friend Michelle spent an extra
night in Cuzco by herself. Being the upstanding
characters that we are, we of course let Kara,
who was cute as hell, hang out with us for the
next couple of days.

There is just no way to accurately describe
the road conditions in Lima. Think of New York
and just keep thinking...Then think much worse.
Lots of horns and cutting in and out. We

witnessed so many horrifying near misses. I still can't believe we avoided seeing a fatality. It got to the point where none of us wanted to ride shotgun. We fought for the backseat.

We managed to land an upscale hotel (a rarity in our travels) in San Isidro called the Regina for $50 USD a room. The hotel was clean and comfortable and even equipped with cable television. It also included a beday if you were so inclined.

We threw our bags down and immediately walked to McDonald's and scored some llama extra value meals. Tasted just like home, gave me the sweaters (diarrhea) and everything...That's how I know it's the same. We hit a few cafés and drank some Bremen and Cristal.

Later on we cruised to the Larcomar, a fancy American-style hangout overlooking the Pacific Ocean. There's a Hard Rock Café, TGI Friday's, Tony Romas, and Kentucky Fried Chicken. All the commercial creations of home. We ate at a place called Manos Morenos (Black Hands). The workers were all black and they dressed like Aunt Jemima. Definitely wouldn't go over well in the States. We ordered crazy dishes off the menu and several rounds of Cristal beer before taking a seat on the plaza. A Japanese guy named June also sat down and asked questions, telling us his living arrangements were pretty bad, just too many Israelis. A theme we kept hearing throughout our visit to Peru. He hung out and talked with us for awhile and smoked about ten cigarettes.

On Monday we headed downtown to check out some sights. We witnessed the changing of the guard at the Governmental Palace at noon. The band played *Hammer and the Nail* by Simon and Garfunkel. Afterwards, we took a tour of the San Francisco Cathedral. It was the first set of catacombs that I had ever toured, although there were a lot of them around in Europe, I had never actually seen them. The mold spores were ever present, but the views were cool, lots of bones and mummies.

We sucked in fumes for the rest of the afternoon, then stopped for a bite to eat at a café, where we were the only patrons, a theme we came across often. We dined on high priced croissants which didn't taste very good. Dusty claims they gave him the gurgles. While eating, a flute player arrived and proceeded to serenade us. We were pretty much tired of people playing instruments, then expecting us to pay them. After all, it wasn't like we asked the old boy to come and serenade us during lunch. The solution was brilliant however. When he came over with his bag open for a tip, Dusty dropped a chocolate cigar from the airplane in his bag. All he could do was smile and go on his way. It was hilarious. I know...A bit sadistic and mean...But hilarious as hell just the same.

Later, we attempted to enjoy a few afternoon cervezas at a little restaurant near our hotel. After ordering a beer, the proprietor, realizing he was out of beer, ran down to the corner store and rustled us up some brew for us. It was a bit on the warm side. Dusty headed to the head with a gurgly stomach and in all the excitement had failed to notice the lack of papel in the banos. He was forced to rip his shirt sleeves off and to use them as substitutes...Such is life on the road...Far, far away from the comforts of one's own abode and comode.

Thus ended our trip to Peru...Probably my favorite place on earth.

Scatpackin' In Desolation Canyon with a Band of Green River Pirates

Utah, 1998

We assembled in Phoenix during the latter part of May. After the ensemble arrived from all over Arizona, we boarded our various vehicles and headed north up I-17 towards Utah and the Green River. There were seven of us: Christian Bates, Dusty Decarlo, Jason Moore, Bruce Gungle, Dale Ward, my brother, Greg "The Fathead" Quinn, and myself. Several others were originally on the list, but "impending doom" swallowed them up. A phrase my dad, Ed "Eddie" Quinn, fashioned for those who drop out of trips at the last minute. Beer weighed heavily on our axles, while the Green River and more specifically, Desolation Canyon, weighed heavily on our minds. Leaving the smog and heat of the Valley of the Sun behind us, we prepared for some adventurous times on the river.

After gassing up with petrol and *Wendy's* grease in Flagstaff, we headed straight for the land of loose horses, stray dogs, corrugated shacks, pickup trucks, satellite dishes, and swaggering gaits...The Navajo Reservation. I truly admire the fact that the Navajos haven't sold out to the casino culture...Not yet anyway...Hope they never do.

We caravanned through Monument Valley in the dark of night, eventually stopping at the town of Mexican Hat to inspect the San Juan River as it rumbled through town. As for the namesake, balancing "Hat" itself, well, let's just say I tried to present it to the gang in all of its fine glory, but all you could really see was the brim's silhouette.

After passing through Blanding and Bluff, Utah in the wee hours of the night, we pulled off down a dirt road and called it a night.

Stars filled the chilly Utah night as our hastily built fire crackled and wisped smoke on up to the Milky Way. It was good to feel so alive and free from life's hassles.

At daybreak...Well, all right...Maybe not quite at daybreak...We rolled through Moab and admired pretty Mormon girls with shiny blonde hair sipping decaffeinated soft drinks. We stopped briefly to admire the Colorado River north of town, then continued on toward our destination of Swasey's Rapid near the town of Green River, Utah. Which was to be our take-out.

Dropping Jay's car, we managed to squeeze into the other two vehicles and begin the seven-hour-long trek to Sand Wash and our put-in point on the river. The road began as a winding, paved route, but after eleven miles, the road changed abruptly to dirt. Lush aspen and pine towered over us. Soldier Creek accompanied us on the side of the road...Or perhaps, the road accompanied Soldier Creek...I'm not sure which description is more accurate. The temperatures were cool and the passengers riding in the back of the pickup trucks prayed for sunshine, as gophers and squirrels looked idly on while we bounced down the rutted road.

Eventually, the landscape on the road changed dramatically. Trees were replaced by rocks. Desolation Plateau is devoid of just about anything but sand and rock. Steep side canyons yawn down into the Green River. We followed the road as it worked its way around each side canyon, one at a time. It was actually very similar to hiking the Tonto Platform in the Grand Canyon where one is basically forced to walk several miles to gain one mile of actual canyon. Every time we rounded the next bend we were convinced a glimpse of the river was imminent, but it wasn't.

Christian, along with Dusty and The Fathead

stopped to check their bearings (or mine) to make sure we were going the right way and suffered a flat tire while turning back around. Not knowing about the flat and thinking they were merely snapping pictures, I continued to drive on. Just about the time we began to become concerned (we had now actually reached Sand Wash and the put-in), a white truck pulled up and asked if we knew some guys in a red Toyota? They said that they had suffered a flat about seventeen miles back and were in need of a four-way lug wrench.

Having procured a wrench from a friendly rafter, I hopped in my truck to retrace my steps back to the Toyota. As I was about to leave, the two good ol' boys in the white truck, one very talkative, the other close-eyed and quiet, informed me that they were heading in that direction and offered to bring the wrench themselves. Sounded good to me.

However, three minutes later, the white truck appeared again and the passenger handed the lug-wrench out the window to me exclaiming "we'd like to help you boys out, but we're on our way to a drug drop, but here's the wrench".

So, wrench in hand, I headed back down the road and Dusty, using his ingenuity, managed to make use of the over-sized semi lug-wrench we had borrowed. Soon afterwards, we were heading back down the road to Sand Wash where we spent the night making final preparations and fending off rabid mosquitoes.

The next morning, which happened to be Memorial Day, we awoke ready to embark on our river odyssey...But first, we had to dispense with the formalities of the official ranger gear inspection. The rangers at the put-in were all about business and were very, very thorough with our belongings and devices.

They "retired" a few of our life jackets or PFD's, stating that when a manufacturers tag is torn, slight or not, that the jacket must be "retired". Even if the jacket is brand spanking new. Sounded like a mattress-tag story to me, but what could we do? We just prayed we still

had enough life jackets to go around after the
final taps were played. I didn't have the
courage to ask where the "retired" life jackets
planned to spend their golden years...And
besides these men were deadly serious about
their job and not willing to take any guff from
a group of simple river running peasants. After
all, it was their damn river and we should just
be gracious for the opportunity to run it at
all!

The inspection and cross-examination
continued and then culminated with the
ScatPacker investigation. Our $135.95 solid
waste receptacle, which consisted of a white
bucket and a nifty screw-down lid, became the
item in question. Such a system is required on
the Green and many rivers throughout the West.
We had forgotten, or purposefully neglected, to
acquire chemical agents to add to the solid
waste, but other than that, it was brand new and
rearin' to be scat in. We would simply have to
endure each other's scattings and go with the
flow...Literally.

We were informed of the dire consequences of
"malicious defecation" and the misdemeanor
nature of this heinous offense that would
ultimately follow us throughout our lives like a
stubborn cling-on. Ranger #1 counted up the
scats and came up with forty-two. His formula
included multiplying the number in our group (7)
by six river days = 42. This formula apparently
didn't account for double dippers or no-
scatters, but it was scientifically calibrated
just the same. Knowing his business in this
very technical area, he had doubts about our
ScatPacker written all over his brow.

"Hmmm, let's see...This particular model is
equipped to house and transport forty uses", he
stated unequivocally. After what seemed like
several very intense moments of contemplation,
he conferred with his associate, Ranger #2, who
without hesitation exclaimed "no problem, it can
be done". We were all quite relieved and
forever indebted to those gentlemen, who found
it in their heart of hearts to let us slide in

51

those extra two shits. I couldn't help but
think how Powell would have embraced the
ScatPacker?

With the investigation...Err...I mean the
Big Brother inquiry completed, our river
adventure officially commenced. The rangers
snickered as we put our (actually my dad's)
small boats in the water. We had a couple of
13-footers and an old ten-foot, non-self-
bailing, barge-like Achilles with a lot of
character. They were small, but we were poised
to make Powell proud. No eighteen-foot fun
islands for us. Of course we didn't own any
eighteen-foot fun islands either, but that was
beside the point.

We launched at 11:13 a.m., local time.
Pretty precise considering river time is
generally not very precise. Not as imprecise as
Peru time mind you...But still not very precise.

Good current and the absence of rapids aided
the first day's mileage. The flows were huge
and hovered around 23,000 cfs (cubic feet per
second). The river had a frothy brown
appearance complete with plenty of wooden
objects from upriver along for the ride. We
paddled fourteen miles and pulled in to camp
above Gold Hole II, which is a rincon. A rincon
being a plot of land formed by a previous
riverbed, which no longer exists.

The sight played host to eight wild horses
and loads of foxtails that wanted to get into
your socks and shoes. Sheer walls loomed
steeply down at us from both sides of the river,
creating a claustrophobic ambiance. We set up
camp beneath box elder and beside poison ivy.
Three members of the party managed to remain-
poison-ivy-free...Four did not.

We drank beer and made various toasts. We
toasted the stockman's skiff left behind in the
bushes from an earlier era. We toasted wild
women, steaks, and scatpackin'. And of course
we toasted Powell.

After devouring juicy chicken fajitas, we
retired to the bushes for sleep and
rejuvenation. Bothered only by a few buzzing

bandits, we located ideal spots in the dirt and began to drift off...But that soon changed, as a cunning menace appeared. We heard the skunk crashing through the weeds and underbrush sounding more like a bear than a skunk. Those of us not snoring heavily, heard him approach and donned flashlights to locate him. Bruce never heard him approach and only got up when he heard me mutter "wow, he's going right for Bruce's head". Upon hearing those words, Bruce sprung to his feet and hastily retreated. Jay somehow slept through the whole skunk encounter, even as my brother threatened to shoot him with his .45 automatic.

The skunk was only the beginning of what turned out to be a most bizarre night. With everyone now wide-awake, we decided to use our buckets for drums and see what kind of echo we could draw from the canyon walls. A few primal screams were also thrown in for good measure.

About an hour later, we encountered hair-raising sounds from both sides of the river. We must have pissed somebody or something off with our echo display. We were unable to locate where the sounds were coming from, or even their nature for that matter. Sheep? Frogs? Cats? None of us had ever heard such a sound. I guess you had to be there to fully appreciate the weirdness of the sounds.

We eventually went back to sleep, only to be awakened an hour or so later by deep kerplunking noises in the middle of the river. First, on the far side and then on our side of the river. It definitely wasn't a beaver smacking his tail. An elk or sheep on top of the ridge could never have propelled a boulder 200 feet out into the river. We were baffled. Perhaps it was Bill the Boulder Thrower, a bigfoot-like creature encountered by Christian and the Fathead on a backpacking trip in the White Mountains of Arizona. *(Editor's note: To this day I haven't been able to explain the sounds or splashes that night on the Green. Nothing made sense. I know it sounds crazy, but to this day, we can all attest to the weirdness that occurred).*

The next day dawned...Without us, as the sun was slow to shine in the deep canyons and alcoves. We shoved off at a casual 11:00 a.m. with only ten miles to log that day. Normally an easy task, but unfortunately Mother Nature had other plans. Upriver winds blew unmercifully all day long, blowing us into the poison-ivy-infested tamarisk growimg on the banks repeatedly.

We camped at Jack Creek, which was akin to camping at a lakeside or even seaside location in the trees. The river, aided by the wind, lapped eagerly on the bank and sounded like waves crashing on an ocean beach. We spent time filtering water out of Jack Creek, which was much clearer than the swollen, muddy Green. Afterwards, we played a little wiffle ball, ate burritos and boasted lies, as all men are wont to do while sitting 'round a roaring fire pan (government regulation all the way).

The following day brought huge waves and just about as much as our poor old ten-foot Achilles raft could handle. The current resembled an ocean, covering most of the rocks and hazards in the river. However, there were huge waves and downside holes to navigate. We crashed up and down standing waves like surfers at Redondo beach. The sixteen-mile run passed by quickly and we soon found ourselves tied in at Rock Creek, which was probably my favorite campsite on the trip.

The banks were lined with large cottonwoods and beyond them lay a field bathed in beautiful red, yellow and purple wildflowers. Wild horses lazed around and grazed at will. Rock Creek thundered down out of the mountains at such a high rate that we had to be very careful while entering it not to get washed downstream into the main channel of the Green. The cliffs beside the creek beckoned us to hike them. So we obliged, climbing up to about 750 feet above the creek and river. The panoramic views of the river and surrounding canyonlands was absolutely dazzling. On the way back down, we hopped over boulders, stopping only momentarily to gaze at our own death falls had we slipped. You definitely didn't want to slip. It would have been a very long time before you saw a hospital.

On the way back to camp we stopped at the "living history museum" on the far side of the meadow. The "museum" was basically a rustic old shack containing late 1800 and early 1900 artifacts. The ranch was built by Dan and Bill Seamounton in the early 1900s. We marveled at the heavy iron machinery and wondered how the hell they ever got it there? It's remains very remote around there today, let alone back then. Transporting those heavy implementations would still be a bitch today. Upon leaving the museum, we had a close encounter with some mule deer and wild horses in the meadow.

While I was busy hiking, Christian was out spotting yet another pair of naked breasts. He has some kind of a pension for spotting naked women. On rivers and in the woods anyway, I don't know about on the street? But, I can't tell you how many times he's come back to camp and told the tale. Usually they belong to a saggy old body, but this time he says they belonged to a fine-looking woman out sunbathing near the creek.

The sun arose on another day of good whitewater and some intense rapids. In the vicinity of Three Fords Rapid, I watched Christian and Bruce, riding in the sleekest boat we had, the Puma, get sucked down into a huge eight to ten foot hole that appeared out of nowhere. He yelled for us to change course, but in the barge-like Achilles...We were committed to our route. We watched as they braved the hole and then rose vertically up and over the crest on the backside. That was promising, but I was very cognizant of the fact that they were in a light boat with larger tubes in comparison to my stout relic with small tubes and a non self-bailing floor.

Dusty and I slid violently down the slide and into the awaiting jaws below. The midstream maelstrom folded up the boat and as we reached a state very near to vertical, I was swept out of the boat into the hole. Dusty, who was still talking to me and pleading for direction, had no idea I was out of the back of the boat until he saw me climb back in. Miraculously I still had the paddle in my hand. With a strong taste of the Green in my mouth, we plowed through the remainder of the rapid, slightly shaken, extremely wet, and truly exhilarated.

We logged twenty miles that day, stopping along the way to visit the McPherson Ranch, which is presently owned by the Ute Indians. Jim McPherson settled at Florence Creek in the 1890s and was often visited by Butch Cassidy and various members of his Wild Bunch. They traded horses and spent time resting at the ranch in between adventures. On one occasion, McPherson asked Wild Bunch member Joe Walker to mind his livestock for him while he went into town. While McPherson was in town, the bank was robbed and the robbery had Joe Walker's signature all over it. When McPherson arrived back at the ranch he confronted Walker about the incident. Walker replied that he had in fact kept his word and watered the stock twice a day, although "it might have been a little early and a little bit late one day. And besides, you didn't tell me what to do with my free time Jim", stated Walker. Walker was later shot in his bedroll on Friday the 13th, 1898, by posse members in the high country east of Florence Creek.

We camped that night at Range Creek, a site dominated by trees, alcoves and plenty of cliffs to climb. Unfortunately, we were greeted by hordes of noseeums or black flies. We discussed Powell and read aloud passages from his journal in which he described some of the places we were enjoying on our trip.

After a river bath, we dined on river-water spaghetti. There's just no substitute for traditional, sand-crunching river-water spaghetti. A must on any trip.

The next day we floated past Curry Canyon and Curry Rapid, which signify the site along the river where "Flat Nose" George Curry was shot down by lawmen April 17th, 1900. Next, we hit the rapids at Coal Creek, which boasts a thundering hole. Thankfully, all three boats managed to avoid the huge hole. We stopped briefly to investigate the ruins of an old stone ranch, which might have been constructed by McPherson, and his offspring, as their names were found on nearby rocks. The site also housed dam workers in 1911.

We planned on camping at Rattlesnake Canyon, but unfortunately while we admiring the scenery, we passed it by. Unable to find a suitable campsite for several miles, we almost ran ourselves out of river, as the take-out was only a few miles away.

Finding a suitable camp, I ordered the *ScatPacker* oficially closed down for health reasons and every man was on his own when it came to such matters. It stunk something aweful. At that point, we definitely could have used the "overlooked" chemicals. But I guess at the time, buying more beer happened to be higher on the priority list. We spent our final night on the river in style, eating and drinking up the remaining provisions. We conducted a Frisbee competition and Dusty flew a kite high above the river.

The next morning we had hardly settled into our paddling routine before we were at the take-out. Jay, Christian and I ran the seven hour shuttle back to Sand Wash as the other guys hung out and waited...Then waited some more...Finding time to dump the *ScatPacker* contents in a J-John. A smelly task.

We picked up a hitchhiking rafter named Tom, who had just completed the same run as we had, only solo, in a fourteen-foot raft. He tipped us off about a great Mexican Restaurant in Moab, where we ran into him later on that evening. And thus ended the legendary journey of the Green River Pirates. I think Powell would have smiled.

The Big Game

Russia, 2001

Soccer. It is one of those sports loved and
revered the world over...Maybe too much for
some, like say the "Hooligans" in England or the
fanatical fans in Colombia who took it upon
themselves to murder the unlucky defenseman that
redirected a shot into his own goal during the
1994? World Cup. In the United States the
appreciation depreciates a bit, as a slight few
love the sport and the many multitudes tend to
despise it. I am one of the few, having played
soccer most of my life religiously. According
to my ex-wife, maybe a bit too religiously, as
in every Wednesday and Sunday all year long here
in Phoenix.

Having been a sports fan for as long as I
dare to remember, I have attended hundreds of
professional games throughout the United States.
Baseball, football, basketball, hockey, and
swamp buggy racing (I had to include you
Southerners). I've witnessed the full spectrum,
from National Championships and playoff games to
dismal 1974 era Cleveland Indian games with a
paltry 3,000 fans scattered throughout old
Municipal Stadium (with a capacity of 80,000).
Where am I going with all this you might ask?
To Moscow of course, for the Big Game.

In 2001, My friend Dusty Decarlo and I
traveled to Russia for a few weeks to explore
Moscow and St. Petersburg. While in Moscow, we
saw an ad for a qualifying match versus
Yugoslavia. We thought what the hell; it should
be entertaining if nothing else. It was
Saturday night and the drinking around Moscow
was in full swing as we entered the subway
station. Although the drinking on Tuesday is

near the same. Oh, why pull punches...There's a
lot of drinking all the time. Cranberry vodka
at the bus stop in the morning, beer at lunch
and vodka shots by evening. I felt drunk just
walking around; no need to feel any more lost.

We had a vague notion of where the stadium
was located. Moscow is an old medieval city
built in concentric rings that move outward from
the city center. Not knowing the language in
Russia is always a slight problem as English is
at a premium and asking questions in English
sometimes gets you nowhere. Not that I'm
complaining mind you, for if a Russian asked me
questions here in America, I probably wouldn't
be much help either.

Luckily, we noticed raucous, patriotic fans
stumbling and parading, waving flags throughout
the subway station. We figured that they knew
where they were headed, so we decided to follow
the crowd.

So, like a couple of Yank lemmings we jammed
into a subway car and waited to see where the
crowd headed. More and more fans came pouring
in at every stop. Each stop became rowdier than
the last. We wondered if we appeared out of
place...Of course we did, but screw it, we were
on our way to the big game. It wasn't like we
were going to root for Yugoslavia, a sure way to
get your head cracked open.

We eventually made it to the stadium stop
and followed the loud revelers up to street
level. There were policeman grabbing people by
the collar and snatching items. Flags,
whistles, bottles, there seemed to be neither
rhyme nor reason. Some items were confiscated,
while somebody right next to them was let
through with that same exact item. I had no
idea if I had "illegal" items or not? I still
don't to this day. Some were running, some
falling, most yelling, many drunk.

We followed blindly to the stadium and
eventually found the correct line to purchase
tickets. No small feat. For those not in tune
to lines, or queues as they are referred to in
many parts of the world, they are definitely

different than what you find in the United States. The line itself is similar, but the lack of personal space is glaring. You might be the last one in a line and someone will come up behind you and sniff your shampoo and crowd your sphincter. An uncomfortable feeling for many Americans, who are used to personal space. Dusty says the Russians should be the kings of the queue, having lined up for so many years under the Soviet system. A system surely missed by many in Russia. "The Soviet times were certain times, now our futures are unknown, and everything is dirty, things were much cleaner before", says Xena, a woman we stayed with in Moscow. Her sentiments are shared by many in Mother Russia.

We finally managed to procure some tickets. They cost 250 rubles each or approximately $7.50 USD. Next we had to make our way into the stadium itself. No small task. We lined up and eventually snaked up to the first checkpoint, not sure exactly what they were checking for. I saw them confiscate everything from flags and bandanas to gum and cigarettes. They felt my pockets and took a few quick glances in my daypack. They never asked me to empty my pockets, they just felt the contents? They nodded us ahead to the next checkpoint, where the ritual repeated itself. And then another and so on. We passed through at least eight or nine of these half-hearted searches, I felt like I was auditioning for the film *Groundhog Day*, starring Bill Murray. Finally, we completed the last checkpoint and were allowed inside. Next, we had to find our seats.

I know what you're thinking....What a trivial set of circumstances. Buying tickets, entering an arena, finding seats. Believe me it was anything but routine and I attend no fewer than 30 professional sporting events a year.

We interpreted the seat numbers on the tickets as well as we possibly could and walked up to the portal matching that description only to be gruffly turned away. A grunt and a nod toward the left. This went on for about fifteen minutes as we traversed the stadium searching for the seats until...You guessed it, we came full circle back to where we started and a different attendant gladly took our tickets.

But not so fast...First another search. We had nothing confiscated during the first nine searches. But this particular policeman took a fancy to my red Bic lighter and decided to commandeer it. Not many Bics in Moscow. Oh well, it could have been worse, like say...My camera. And what exactly could I do about it anyway, complain at the customer relations kiosk?

So there we were, down near the field, fans packed into 1970s era, multi-colored, red, yellow, and blue plastic seats. You might have thought a beer or at least a pop was in order. Perhaps some nachos or a big pretzel. That wasn't happening. Everyone had purposely tanked up on the way to the stadium. Inside there were no kiosks with food, drinks, or trinkets to be found. Later on, I was told the rationale, or at least that person's rationale...That items would only become projectiles intended to be thrown onto the field and therefore they were forbidden.

However, fireworks must not have been covered under this ruling, as Roman candles, bottle rockets, and firecrackers erupted from all points within the stadium. Cops chased, grabbed, and beat down people throughout the arena. I was also told that the added security, which was evident everywhere inside the facility (perhaps four thousand civil and military personnel), was in place in case the Chechens were wont to act out in violence.

A word about the "Chechen problem". To discuss the situation in Chechnya with Russians can be a very lively event. First the jaw drops, then the brow furrows, after which an unkind word is soon to follow. Like an exuberant "*#&@&^%! criminals", for instance. If you were to say something like "why not just let them break away?"...A response akin to: "Would you just let California or New York just break away, I think not", is sure too follow. I find myself pausing for a few awkward seconds while contemplating my response to the California/New York secession.

Ironically enough, I play soccer with a great group of Russians every Sunday. They hail from all over the former Soviet Union: Uzbekistan, Ukraine, Georgia, Moscow, St. Petersburg, Siberia, to name a few. And the heated Chechen subject has come up on more than one occasion. "Now you've done it", is the most memorable response I can recall. As if I had just opened a huge can of ugly worms or drank someone's last sip of vodka. I can't deny the fact that Chechens have committed terrorist acts in Moscow, but it seems to me that they are to blame for everything from the economy to weather. All right, enough about those "heathen" Chechens and back to the Big Game.

We were now inside, minus a red Bic lighter, but otherwise intact. The game itself was an important qualifier; thus the excitement level was intense. People yelled, screamed, blew whistles and set bottle rockets off.

A ways after halftime we decided that leaving a little early might be the intelligent thing to do. After all, we followed the crowd in and really hadn't paid much attention to the stops. It was also getting dark (this was Moscow after all and not St. Petersburg where it remains light practically all damn night long) and we just wanted to beat the rush and retrace our steps.

We walked down the ramp to the exit turnstiles, and attempted to leave. An usher at the exit held up his hands in a stop-right-there-where-the-hell-do-you-stupid-Americans-think-you-are-going position. We executed our best gestures to emulate leaving the stadium, but he just shook his head. I thought maybe that wasn't the exit? Let's try the next exit...No, not there either. We walked halfway around the stadium and were stonewalled at every turn.

We stood and thought about the matter at

hand. We began rationalizing. We weren't
trying to get in, we were merely trying to
leave. We didn't want any money back; we simply
wanted to leave the stadium. I thought maybe
they thought (and that's a lot of thinking) we
wanted to leave and then reenter, so I gestured
and mumbled..."Leave, no come back". But even
this tactic received a grunt and a stiff shake
of the head.

A couple of guys overheard our plight and
asked if we wanted to leave. Yes, we wanted to
leave, we explained. He explained this to the
usher, but the usher still refused. Then a
smiling cop overheard and the story was repeated
again. He laughed and laughed? Then he asked
if we wanted to leave and we shook our heads in
the affirmative. Yes, we wanted to leave. He
then asked for money and I don't know if he was
kidding or not, because his facial expression
never changed. He possessed an unfailing shit-
eating-grin at all times. We just laughed an
uncertain laugh and he let us out of the pen we
were in. We never did pay him any rubles.

Tasting freedom, we walked towards the
subway station, stopping to purchase a Russian
jersey on the way. As we rounded the last bend
toward the Metro we came upon a site to behold.

A gauntlet line was amassed composed of two
solid lines of police officers in full riot
gear, complete with shields, helmets, billy
clubs, tear gas, dogs, horses, and machine guns.
We walked down the middle of the two columns all
the way to the station. Probably routine to the
Russians, but definitely foreign to us. Very
intimidating to say the least. I would have
actually liked to stick around and watch the
crowd funnel down the five-foot wide gauntlet
line. It must have been something to see? But
instead we rode the subway back to our gracious
host Xena's flat and discussed life in the
Soviet times, before that wretched thing called
free enterprise reared its ugly head.

The Doka Incident

Arizona, 1991

February in Arizona. Weather just doesn't
get much better. Camping time in the desert.
Even the rattlesnakes are a little nicer. A
small group of us decided to head out to the
Verde River for a relaxing break from the
everyday grind. Maybe a little bit of hiking,
target shooting, and barbequing. No stress...No
worries. I joined Jeff "Clarence" Linssen and
his wife (she is no longer and therefore will
remain unmentioned), Clarence's sister Vicki and
her man at the time (Chris something?) and Ray
"The Gamblin' Man" Legenzoski in the town of
Fountain Hills.

After driving on dirt roads for about half
an hour, we found a spot on the river that was
absolutely gorgeous and perfect in every
facet...Well almost...It would have been had it
not been located on the Fort McDowell Indian
Reservation. Plenty of trees and shade
overlooking the river on a steep, twelve-foot
bank. Lush desert all around us, full of
healthy saguaros, cholla, yucca, and ocotillo.
The place seemed ideal for our purposes.

We didn't like the idea of being on
reservation land, but figured we were way off
the beatin' path and on the opposite bank from
the residential areas and most importantly the
bingo casino (today they have a "real" Indian
casino). Ray and I went out chasing rabbits
around the desert while everyone else hung
around camp and did their thing. A few hours
later, back at camp, we encountered an unwelcome
interloper from across the river.

How the guy spotted us I'll never know.
Maybe he smelled the food or most probably the

liquor. The first time I saw Doka, he was armpit deep in the river and coming our way (keep in mind it was February and the river was running high and bitterly cold with snowmelt). The uninvited crossing signaled the beginning of the end of our paradisiacal day.

Upon approaching our side of the river, the soaked, inebriated, Indian in raggedy clothing attempted to climb up the steep bank to our camp. He rolled down into the river a few times, finally making it up on his third attempt. He said his name was Sergeant Doka and then tried telling us he was a member of the tribal police, but that didn't get him very far...His entrance didn't help his ruse out any.

Truth be known, if we hadn't had been on reservation land, we probably would have run the soggy, lyin', son of a bitch out immediately...But, unfortunately we didn't. Now, I know what you're probably thinking...These assholes sure aren't hospitable hosts. We are, I just don't like being shined on that's all.

Clarence offered the Dokster a pull on his whiskey bottle and the one pull became many pulls until it was damn near empty. Then some beers for good measure, followed by Vicki's vodka. He staggered around telling us how he killed "lots of fuckin' gooks" in Vietnam (unfortunately, he was far too young to have served in Vietnam). He said he was admired by all of his subordinates and the most loved sergeant in the Army. "Nobody gave me any shit", he exclaimed.

After a short while, I decided that I had enough of Doka. Ray and I walked over by my truck and went about setting up a few targets for the .22 rifle. A short while later, Doka stumbled over and asked if he could shoot at the targets. I didn't really want to let him, but stupidly, I did anyway.

He shot wildly and missed all the targets. He was convinced that he hit some of them however and walked up to see for himself. He walked passed the targets and up the hill beyond. Ray and I looked at each other "like what the hell is this guy doing"? He got to the top of the rise and I asked him where he was going (he still had my rifle in his hand). "I'm looking for rabbits and squirrels to shoot at", he replied. I wasn't happy about it, but wasn't really overly concerned either. I mean it wasn't like he was going to steal my gun or anything...Was he? After a brief moment on the hill, he descended down the other side and out of our view. I recall Ray and I looking at each other and laughing, as if to say is this really happening, is he really trying to steal the rifle? No...He really couldn't be that brazen could he? After all, we all had handguns holstered to us and I even had a scattergun leaning on the truck next to me. Nobody in their right mind could be that damned brazen!

The Gamblin' Man and I waited about two minutes for him to come back over the hill, then sprinted up ourselves. He was gone...Vanished. I couldn't believe my own eyes. No way this guy could have run, or better yet, wobbled, off with my rifle. We were more than generous...Way more than generous to this guy. Alcohol, food, cigarettes, target shooting...Now this? No way.

I can honestly say I became a bit incensed at that point. My blood was boiling. I ran back down to the truck and grabbed my shotgun and yelled over to Clarence to grab his gun and be on the lookout for a runaway renegade with an M-16-looking .22 rifle. My first instinct was to run toward the river and block an escape by water. Nothing. We decided to fan out and walk away from camp slowly. I remember asking myself "how far could a blitzed guy in his condition have gotten in two or three minutes"?

After searching for about fifteen minutes, Ray and I spotted him below us in some bushes trying to hide out. With his back to us and Ray's laser sight trained on the back of his head, I yelled for him to come out of the bushes. At first he didn't move. Maybe he thought he was camouflaged or some silly thing like that? Even though I was extremely pissed off, I was more worried that Ray might pop a .22 round into the Dokster. He might force our hand.

We decided that if he wheeled around and shot at us, we would have no choice but to shoot him? It wasn't worth the hassle, but I sure as hell wasn't going to let him shoot me either. All we could do was hope he came to his senses. And if not, there was a nice cut bank that could be stomped down on top of him. He could rest eternally. It was his choice. Fortunately, he decided to give up. We eased down to him and marched him back to camp with his hands behind him, shotgun to his head.

I know...Way too mellow-dramatic, but man, was I pissed off. Clarence was deathly afraid I was going to shoot him or at the very least, pummel him. I somehow refrained. It seemed that while he was out "shooting rabbits", he somehow found the time to deeply carve the inscriptions "Sgt. Doka" on one side of my rifle stock and "coyote", apparently his old Army nickname, on the other side with a rock.

Interestingly enough, Doka had the audacity to think that he could continue to hang out with us and that everything would be fine. Maybe if we provided a beer or two for him everything would just work its way out. "How 'bout a pretzel", he asked? Incredulous, we motioned toward the river and watched without ceremony as the leech slowly waded across and out of our lives.

Unfortunately, the day was pretty much ruined. Tensions were high, and I didn't want to take any chances of him coming back with others in tow. Possibly even the tribal police, which might have ended up being the guy's brother-in-law.

After an ugly argument between Ray and Clarence about leaving, we left our perfect spot on the Verde and headed back to the city. Is there a lesson to be learned from all of this? Yes...Don't camp out on reservation land and if you do...Don't dare feed the animals.

Tugging the Rug

Morocco, 1997

Sometime in Germany, Dusty Decarlo and I decided we needed to travel to the Rock of Gibraltar. I don't really know why? But no sooner had we said it, than I knew we were headed that way. We wanted to check out the Barbary Apes that resided on the "Rock". I figured that the Prudential Insurance Company had exploited Americans for years with the image of the Rock of Gibraltar. Perhaps, we might do some exploiting and get a little piece of the rock for ourselves. And I don't mean Rock Hudson. On the twelve-hour train trip down from Barcelona to Algericas, Spain, we decided that a visit to Tangiers, Morocco would also be in order.

In Algericas, a bustling little port town built on the side of a hill which rolled down to the sea below; we inquired about buses to Gibraltar and ferries to Morocco. With only a couple of days remaining on our six-week Europe odyssey, we had to decide which destination appealed more to us...Apes...Or...Africa. Africa won out and after stashing our packs in lockers at the train station, we headed down to the ferry for our trip across the Straits of Gibraltar to Tangiers.

We sauntered down the steep, haphazard, cobbled streets to the sparkling blue sea below and found the ferry waiting at the pier. It was warm and I felt the crazy urge to run off the pier and dive headlong into the enticing ocean. We were herded into a queue (line) and made to march past a small window manned by bored Spanish customs officials, who glanced with

disinterest at our passports. Stamping the
passports, they waved us through. Passing by
several toothless Arabs haggling in the street,
we boarded an old ship and climbed to the
topmost deck for the 2 1/2-hour sailing to
exotic Tangiers.

There we were, standing atop a rusty old
ship gazing out upon the beautiful topaz waters
below where the Atlantic met the Mediterranean
Sea.

On board, we ran into several other
backpackers making their way across to Morocco.
Several Aussies and several Canadians, along
with a high-on-himself Clevelander who wasn't
representing my birthplace well at all. We
talked and watched crews working in the harbor,
busily offloading containers from all over the
world. As we passed by the "Rock" we knew that
that would be as close as we came to touching it
on the trip. There was always next time.

We ate French Bread and chocolate generously
supplied by two Canadian sisters named Nicole
and Lisa, who were making their way to Fez and
Marrakech. Brave women for sure. A group of
Spanish tourists amused us by posing for
snapshots in front of a naked maiden statue on
the deck. They must have snapped a full roll of
pictures of themselves intertwined between and
among the maiden's blossoming anatomy. Each was
trying to outdo the previous friend's sexually-
explicit pose.

Clambering downstairs to have our passports
stamped, we witnessed swarthy figures swaying to
the beat of *Cherish the Love*, which was replayed
no less than eight times in a row over the
ship's crackling loudspeakers.

As the hazy outline of Morocco came into
view, *Cherish the Love* was abruptly substituted
for a wild Arabic beat and the ambiance changed
completely. The chaotic Arabic beat perfectly
foreshadowed and encapsulated the perverse
rhythm of Tangiers.

The mountainside city of Tangiers came
gradually into focus before us. White adobe
buildings piled endlessly on top of each other

all the way down to the water's edge. Swarms of market day inhabitants filled the alleyways and cobbled streets of the medina. It gave me the impression of a great white ant hill...Minus the a queen ant to tell them what to do. There appeared to be a frantic, chaotic, disorderly order to the place.

Disembarking, we were immediately pounced on by "official tour guides" offering sightseeing services, their gold teeth reflecting in the bright sunshine. Mad, dark-skinned carnies grabbed our arms and tryed to lead us off on their tour. Those not trying to sell us a tour were busy trying to sell us hashish and heroin. They offered their services in Spanish Pesetas, French Francs, German Marks, or U.S. Dollars, but they certainly didn't want anything to do with Moroccan Dirhams, their own native currency. Personal space being a distant afterthought, I could literally smell, if not taste, the Moroccan diet.

After being jostled about for several anxious moments, we decided to hire Ammen, who repeatedly warned us that our newfound friends from the ship would be wont to get us into all sorts of trouble in Tangiers. He said they would be searching for and taking part in wild orgies of hashish and marijuana, eventually winding up in a dark, dank, Moroccan jail. Well, I don't doubt the reputation of the jails, but the so-called "hippies" weren't leading us to any place we weren't going ourselves. And I sure as hell didn't need any drugs to stimulate me. Tangiers is all the stimulation anyone ever needs. It's one big psychedelic trip in and of itself. But, we were on a day trip and the rest of the gang was heading inland, so we said our farewells and headed off with Ammen into the madding, crowded streets.

It was 1997, and Saddam had reared his ugly head again, promising death to Americans. We were after all in a Muslim country and several days prior, a bus carrying fifty-five tourists in Egypt was blown to bits on a city street by extremists. If there was any consolation, a

U.S. Destroyer lay docked just off the coast. The destroyer was in Morocco to celebrate the day that Morocco recognized the Declaration of Independence. It was such a sweet feeling knowing they were there for us in our time of need.

The soldiers were all dressed in civvies for security reasons. However, they still stuck out like sore thumbs and were obviously bigger targets than us.

Ammen it turned out was very intelligent and answered my many, crazy comments and questions about politics, religion, culture, and toilets as best he could. He wore a long, flowing, tan robe along with wild, colorful running shoes. The two styles clashed awfully, but then who the hell am I to comment, having no fashion sense whatsoever myself. He explained that he was a distance runner and he even showed us his trophies to prove it.

We toured the Kasbah, high on a cliff overlooking the ocean and the local dump below. The Kasbah was crumbling slowly back into its former self...Dust. But I guess we all are. Ammen was quick to prevent us from taking the unsavory scenic overlook tour. We watched in complete horror as several tourists stood unwittingly smoking and laughing on a parapet of death several hundred feet above the crashing waves and trash below. The structure they were standing on, balancing precariously on a strand of rebar. From our high vantagepoint, the Forbes mansion and Club Med were visible down the beach and far away from the hustle and bustle of the city.

We visited bakeries and butcher shops, with decaying meat hanging idly in the midday heat beside chickens way past their prime. We toured several mosques, which were segregated by sex. I watched in sad dismay as "teachers" instructed their students on the finer points of rug weaving at the "school". The "school" was located in a dark, windowless, hovel with a dirt floor. Five-year olds were busy at work in the sweatshop. A scene right out of *Oliver Twist*.

71

While walking through the narrow, twisting corridors that passed for streets, we were forced to take a detour, as two bloody competitors desperately clawed at each other. "Probably drank too much wine or perhaps smoked too much hashish", informed Ammen. I kept expecting an angry Ali Baba figure to appear from a doorway, waving a dastardly, insane-looking Moorish scythe at us. I had already witnessed his Forty Thieves back at the ship. Where the hell was Indiana Jones when you really needed him anyway?

To the market we marched. Toothless beggars and destitute business-types wallowing beneath ratty tents plying their wares. Everything from used batteries to bottled water complete with a greenish tint, freshly-filled from the fountain in the town square. I know...I watched a woman fill them. We spotted tattered, "like new" AC/DC concert shirts, that were apparently purchased from "good-will" type agencies in the States. Rusty chains, odd nuts and bolts, fly-encrusted candy, old buttons, nifty 1970 era tennis shoes, huge loaves of rounded breads, transistors, slightly used underwear and on and on and on...Quite a mind-blowing experience...Like I said earlier, who the hell needed any drugs to feel buzzed?

Women in shawls looked at us with an air of curiosity and distaste. I kept wondering what the hell they really looked like underneath their veils. I also wondered what they thought about? Were they happy?

We passed a man madly chopping away at a cow's femur bone with a huge machete. He busily collected the shavings. For what reason? I could only imagine. The Naval band struck up patriotic tunes before a glum, expressionless crowd that appeared to melt beneath the blue African sky. We walked on in a somewhat dreamlike fashion, our savior Ammen whisking away unsavory characters that approached us with a wave of his robed arm. He continued to smile and greet friends in the endless see of faces.

As we walked, I asked Ammen if it was always

as crazy as it appeared to me at that moment.
"No...Not always". By the way he paused, I
could tell he was lying. It was always that
crazy. And at times, crazier. Like when the
pagan Muslims began hitting the hash pipe and
consuming large quantities of cheap wine.

Eventually, Ammen led us to a large three-
story adobe building. The place dwarfed the
modest hovels around it. We followed him inside
and were immediately "graced" by the presence of
several businessmen. This particular
establishment dealt in rugs, jewelry, clothing,
trinkets, and probably lots of other items that
lurked out of our immediate view. We were
escorted upstairs to the rug room. A monstrous
room filled with rugs of every size, shape, and
design imaginable.

Ammen said that he had to go pray and my
heart immediately sank into my stomach. He left
us with a father and son combination in pointy
shoes and matching grins. We knew the scene.
The little stop on the tour was pre-planned and
Ammen received a kickback for bringing unwary
foreigners into the lion's den so to speak. I
knew we would have to buy something...Or else.

I thought we caught a break when the
loudspeakers outside began crackling with the
eerie-sounding prayers broadcast from the
muezzin. I politely excused myself so that the
two proprietors could partake in their holy
duties. "Noooo...Business first", however, was
the reply I received from the pair as two *Orange
Fantas* arrived, served to us by a young waiter.
"All Americans drink *Fanta*", exclaimed the older
pointy-toe. "They sure do", I replied, while
trying to keep a straight face. I tried to
remember the last time I sucked down one of the
tasty orange delights. Unfortunately, Dusty's
Fanta bottle had a chipped top and not knowing
if the piece was inside or lying on the ground
somewhere, he sipped very carefully. At this
point you might be asking yourself why we didn't
ask for another *Fanta*? Believe me...Had you
been in our shoes...In that place...You wouldn't

have asked either. In America sure...But we
sure as hell weren't in America. Not by a long
shot.

After the drinks, came the business at hand.
An employee or three of the pointy-toes began to
roll out one rug after the next. They came
crashing down with a Wwwhhhhuuummpp sound that
I'll never, ever forget. The room had a very
distinctive aroma to it, not really unpleasing,
but very hard to describe. With each new rug
that was unfurled, the tension level seemed to
grow, as the younger pointy-toe lit cigarettes
and threw them down on the rug to show us their
fire-retardant nature...I guess?

I knew we would have to buy a rug. The
younger pointy-toe courted Dusty to the far side
of the rug room as the older pointy-toe
whispered his bargains in my ear. I finally
caved in and agreed to buy a small cashmere rug.
I could see by Dusty's body language that he was
relieved, as he now figured he was off the hook
since one of us had made a purchase. Don't get
me wrong, the rugs were beautiful. But I have
serious problems with five-year-old laborers.
And besides, we were traveling light and I
didn't want to carry around a damn rug.

So, after exchanging Spanish pesetas with
the rug dealers that amounted to about $40 USD,
we were *allowed* to leave, but not before
inspecting the various wares downstairs. I
briefly imagined carting a large sword through
customs, maybe even wearing it on my hip while
walking around downtown Lisbon.

We found Ammen waiting outside with a
sheepish, guilty look on his face. We exchanged
glances and sensing I wasn't very happy, he
apologized. It was hard for me to be that angry
though. After all, he had to stay in
Tangiers...I got to leave.

After several more sights, we headed back to
the ship for our return journey to Spain.
Darkness enveloped the city as we climbed to the
top of the ship and looked out over the lights
of Tangiers. We smoked an Indian and began
laughing out loud. The stressors of the day

leaving our tired bodies.

Back in Algericas, we followed signs on benches and on the side of buildings to a *McDonald's*, where we ordered a couple of *Big Mac* value meals...Mine with a beer in the place of a *Coke*. Unfortunately, while opening my pesky ketchup packet, I managed to knock over my beer into Dusty's lap. He was pissed off, but all I could do was laugh and apologize. And then laugh some more. He couldn't get his ketchup open either. Damn those incompetent ketchup manufacturers!

It was now around midnight and nearly everything in town was closed. We had to navigate through the maze of streets back up the hill to the train station, where our backpacks were stashed in the lockers. We walked around in circles for awhile, even stopping to ask directions at a police station. The cops just laughed at us while grabbing their huge bellies. I didn't think it was that funny. I was even speaking Spanish. Eventually, we found the station. It was dark, really dark. There was a little guard shack out front with a napping old guard inside. We inquired about the lockers and the guard just repeated "manana, manana", over and over again.

Moving on without our packs, we rented a pension for the night. Taking cold showers, we were obliged to wear the same smelly, sweaty clothes on our backs. We finally fell asleep dreaming of rugs, robes, and transistors across the Straits of Gibraltar.

The Inhospitable Hostel

England, 1997

Saying goodbye to my cousins Pat and Becky Faith in the Irish harbor town of Dun Laoghaire, my friend Dusty Decarlo and I jumped on an eastbound ferry across the Irish Sea to Holyhead, Wales. The *Stena Liner* was more than accommodating and the trip across was uneventful aside from the endless stream of scam artists attempting to get your boarding pass. I actually gave mine to a woman, not knowing the rationale behind her desire to acquire the pass in the first place. Apparently there's a limit to the amount of beer and cigarettes that an individual can purchase with each pass. Thus, the more passes one possesses, the more one can acquire. So I lost the pass, but wasn't planning to buy anything anyway, so no great loss. Although, the learning curve did come into play the next time, as I became much more wise to the ploy in similar situations in the future.

After pulling into Holyhead, we headed to the train station to await a train bound for London. While waiting (something you do a lot of when traveling), we met up with two Aussies who were returning from "holiday" in Ireland named Stu and Miles. They related wild stories of drunken-sex-orgies and sleeping on park benches. Who knows how much was really true? Actually, they were quite entertaining. Strine has to be the most comical English dialect, with those hilarious slang syllables oozing out in every phrase.

With some embarrassment, they offered us a Foster's Lager. They said they despised the beer touted in the States as "Australian for

Beer". Stu said that Foster's was synonymous with shit in Australia and that it was the equivalent of Hamm's, Blatz or Keystone in the States. Apologies to those of you sipping one of those fine beers as you peruse this crummy book. The Aussies said it was the only beer available on the *Stena Liner*, so they just had to go with the Foster's...Or face the dire, unthinkable task of going without. We appreciated the Foster's just the same, even though it was warm. It really hit the spot.

Stu was visiting from Melbourne and was preparing to leave for South Africa in a few days. He possessed a round-the-world pass, which is a great buy for those with a lot of time to spare. Miles, who was actually a dual citizen (Great Britain and Australia), ran a youth hostel in the suburb of Brixton. He invited Dusty and I back to his hostel, a kind gesture given we had no reservations. We normally like to take it day by day. It makes things more authentic and adventurous that way...Sometimes maybe a bit too adventurous.

Miles assured us that the location of his hostel in Brixton was "the place to be". He said that Brixton was "an up and comer" in London and that this "groovy" place was destined to be "sheik" in five years' time and that now was definitely the time to invest. At the time, I might have given him a dollar for the whole damn borough. However, having met several Brits in South America and subsequently staying with them in Brixton on my way back from Russia in 2001, I can honestly say the place has boomed since my first encounter. I still wouldn't live there. Electric Avenue or not. However, real estate prices have risen, so I hope Miles invested some dough himself.

After arriving at Euston Station in London, we were thankful just to have some company and a place to stay for the night...Or so we thought anyway. We boarded the famed *Tube* and took a twenty-minute ride underground to fabled Brixton. I remember standing in the crowded train taking in the sights and sounds, which are of course routine for the residents, but actually pretty bizarre to an outsider looking in. People of all walks, shapes, colors and origin jumped on and off. Some sang tunes, some tried to read, others slept. I am always thoroughly amazed by the sleepers on any given subway throughout the world. How they wake up at their stop, I'll never know. But sleep they do, in New York, London, Moscow, and Kuala Lumpur. The whole subway experience reminds me of rhythmic chaos. It's a sociologist's dream and an agoraphobic's nightmare. I found myself digging it and hating it at the same time. The riders all appeared to be in their own distant worlds, minding their own business...Unconnected and unaffected. So close, yet so very, very far away. Cold, frowning rats, drowning in their own *Herbatrail* of life, swearing expletively that they really do like living this way.

We popped up for air at the Brixton station, which may have been confused for East Los Angeles, South Chicago, East St. Louis, East Cleveland, or any other run-down, seedy locale. The heavy-handed hints of crime and poverty blended harmoniously with passing taxicabs and biting winds. Bobbies with billyclubs glared at us with contempt as we humped our heaping, ungainly, turtle shells down their mean streets with uncertain grins on our faces.

We followed the Aussies for several blocks to the hostel. The place was signified with a welcoming proclamation: **Raleigh Gardens...We have free toilet paper!** Well, it was sure as hell no peach, but a beggar can't complain.

The first several hours were a real blast. We sat around in the cramped office stuffed with backpacks and crummy old furniture and discussed past and future adventures. The various employees there at the Gardens had been all over the world and I listened intently, as I always do...Trying to learn more.

Miles assured us he'd look into vacancies and if none were to be had, we were welcome to crash on the floor, which by the way was just fine with Dusty and I. All was grand until around 11 p.m., when Miles found some accommodations for us upstairs.

We climbed a creaky, narrow staircase past a makeshift kitchen and a filthy, (and I mean filthy, not just untidy) bathroom to a room on the third floor. We encountered a most horrifying scene: An obese woman with multitudes of nodules protruding from her pasty-white face, dressed in black, busily splotching dabs of adobe mud on her face before a cracked mirror in preparation for who only knew what? She was seated at a cluttered card table surrounded by pans of crusty, three-day-old spaghetti O's, scid-marked-scivvies, yellowing newspapers, a mound of cigarette butts, and bottles of various shape and size. We offered a polite hello, but received only our own echo in return. She didn't even bother to turn around and acknowledge that we came into the room. Dusty and I just looked at each other and shrugged our shoulders, trying our best not to laugh.

Apparently, many of the "guests" were on the long-term plan, staying for weeks or even months. Maybe she was pissed off that Miles sent people up to *her room*. I have no idea. I would have rather slept on the ratty office floor downstairs. In all honesty, it would have been cleaner and quieter.

We investigated our sleeping quarters, which consisted of a bunk bed rising out from a pile of filthy clothes and miscellaneous items below. Dusty took the bottom and I, the top. The first thing we did, following our wise, traveling custom, was to dispense with the top cover. This article of bedding is seldom, if ever washed at hotels, and at the Gardens, probably was never washed. After throwing the smelly, you-know-what-stained sheets and comforter on the floor with all the other disgusting articles of clothing and candy wrappers, we threw our sleeping bags down on the concave mattresses. I always find it more comforting to have my own filth wrapped around me instead of someone else's.

After situating our meager possessions, we

headed across the street for some *Big Macs* from a *McDonald's* that might have passed for one in Johannesburg, as Zulu, rather than English, was definitely the language of choice.

Upon returning to the hostel, we again attempted to break the ice with the woman in black, but were rebuffed once more. I thought maybe she had been preparing to go out, but that's what I get for thinking. Tired as hell, we jumped (very carefully) into the concave bunks, to attempt anyway...To sleep.

Sleep was long in coming, as all the lights in the room illuminated down upon us. It was well past midnight by now, as the television hanging from the ceiling blared intently. Meanwhile, the beauty queen kept at it with the makeup. Believe you me, it would have taken more than mud and *Maybelline*...

I think I started to finally go under an hour or so later, when another character suddenly entered the room and awoke me. I had to shake the cobwebs of exhaustion from my head to realize that the person talking was in fact real and that I wasn't dreaming. An effete-looking cat, dressed in black and adorned with many piercings below a half-shaven head of black locks entered and immediately struck up a loud conversation with the witch. I think they were purposely loud, deciding that we were merely a pair of interloping bums in *their* room. At least they turned the blaring tele off. The conversation ensued, and sometime into it...I fell back asleep.

In the predawn hours of Brixton, I was again pulled from slumber to the sound of whisperings that weren't exactly whispers. This time it was a Danish girl in her mid-twenties with blond hair and clad in black. It took me a full half-hour of misery to come to the conclusion that she was a woman. For the life of me I thought perhaps Robert Plant had made a slummish call to Brixton to visit the witch and the transvestite. Either way, the song did in fact remain the same...More loud discussion and little chance for any sleep.

"Robert" woke up "Broomhilda" under the guise of the all too familiar phrase: "Hey, I gotta tell you a really quick story". Nine times out of ten a "really quick story", is anything but. Unfortunately, this was no exception, and I became their captive audience, unable to escape my sagging-bed predicament. Apparently, "Robert's" ex-boyfriend wanted to call some sort of a meeting between his ex-Danish girlfriend "Robert" and his new "thang" (which I can only imagine). After smoothing things over, the ex-boyfriend wanted to know if the "former" was into a threesome with the "new" and himself. I never did hear the answer. I must have drifted back off...Shucks

We awoke to a pitiful shower experience, complete with mildew and the absence of a showerhead. On the bright side there was lukewarm drizzle falling quickly out of the appliance.

After a little laundry duty across the street, we checked out from what would become our only hostel experience in Europe and headed across the English Channel to Calais, France, where we had planned to sleep on the beach.

Planned, being the operative word here. It was a bit cold and industrial in Calais by the sea. Instead, we wandered aimlessly for a few hours laden with heavy packs through a dark, inactive, shut-down town, before finding accommodations in a nauseatingly hot room with a blasting heater that had no off button. I probably would have gone out of my mind had it not have been for the over-priced *Jupiler* beers from a nearby cafe'. Who ever said the French can't help out an American in need?

Gone Flushing...

Arizona, 2003

Oh the things we Americans take for granted.
You know the saying; "it's the little things in
life, that matter." Things like showers and
toilets are far, far from your mind as you plan
a trip to a foreign land. Here's a word of
advice: Bring plenty of papel. Otherwise, you
just might find yourself in the awkward position
of ripping your shirtsleeves off in a cafe' (As
my friend Dusty can attest to). I know what
some of you are thinking. "Look, I've been on
plenty of vacations in the United States with
sub-par, maybe even disgusting service station
or restaurant bathrooms. Shoe-stickin', drafty,
greazzy, stall-doorless, cramped-for-space,
overflowing affairs." Yeah, but I bet there
were no signs telling you to please place your
toilet paper in the rubbish basket next to the
commode. An unfortunate fact of life in many
European and Latin American locales. And, I
don't just mean in run down establishments, but
in many, many establishments.
Whether you call them restrooms, banos,
WC's, loo's, dunny's or tualets, you are sure to
find yourself scratching your head at some
point. You may find yourself contemplating
(perhaps swearing softly) just how the bloody
thing works, or if it ever worked in the first
place? You might even wonder if plumbing had
been invented? I can only speak for myself, but
I never get much rest in a public restroom.
Always a bit nerve wracking. Always someone
trying to jiggle the door handle or something.
What's the deal with seat less toilets?
There are always holes tapped and milled for the
seat to attach, yet the seat itself is absent.
Who the hell wants to squat on a seat less
toilet some guy just pissed all over? You don't

want to do that at your own house, let alone in public. Is it really that much more expensive to buy a toilet with the seat attached? Apparently so.

In Morocco, you might have the occasion to visit a toilet whereby you place your feet on slanted pedals and attempt to hit the bullseye...A small hole, below. In Peru, you might just encounter a stall with a small hole in the center, but no pedals to slant on. Or perhaps a seat less toilet with no flushing mechanism at all. Or perhaps an old plastic bucket beside some ancient, rusty oil drum as the flusher.

In Singapore, which is a very modern, ascetically clean place to be sure, you'll find curious-looking (well, they sure were curious to me anyway) stalls containing squatting pans. These consisted of raised platforms set on a downward angle to a drain at the far end where a man or I suppose a woman (remember, I *was* in the men's restroom) squats and relieves him or herself. Admittedly, I never actually utilized this contraption, and *of course*, I never peeked at anyone else in the act either.

Unless you have stayed at a posh hotel in the U.S., you may not have had the pleasure (I guess it's a pleasure anyway) of having a beday in your bathroom. This form of toilet is equipped with a jet stream of warm water and is positioned adjacently to the "regular toilet". The idea is to do your business, then hop over to the beday for a rinse. Washcloths are placed in the ready, in order to dry off. Just don't mistake *that* washcloth for the one you plan to wash your face with.

In fact, many hotels (at least the crummy places *I tend* to stay at) don't offer washcloths at all, so maybe nobody confuses the two? Two things extremely hard to find in Europe: Washcloths and big cookies. I have always ignored the beday myself, but my friend Dusty did employ one in Portugal and found it to be "downright refreshing".

A most bizarre practice occurs on trains,

where you flush (usually using a foot pedal) right down on the passing rails below. Thus the signs reading: **Absolutely no flushing at the station**. The first time I witnessed this, I was in Italy. I flushed and then to my surprise watched as the bottom slid open and revealed passing slats at sixty miles an hour. My traveling companions didn't believe me and had to go test the system out for themselves. They returned laughing and very much convinced. In Malaysia, the train WC, or restroom, was equipped with a hose sprayer, somewhat akin to a dish sprayer in your kitchen. I'm glad I didn't have to put that one to use! By the way there was no toilet paper, just another reason to bring your own. Or else, I guess you might just have to go with the flow...Literally.

Showers, although nowhere near as comical, have their own idiosyncrasies. First off, a warm shower, let alone a hot shower, is a notable enigma in much of the world. Some hotels, in Bolivia for instance, advertise certain hours (10 a.m.-2 p.m.) in which you might obtain warm water. However, for the most part it is really hit and miss and more often than not...Miss.

Jump in, bare your teeth, and tough it out. At least some hotels will be honest with you right up front and simply convey the fact to you that under no circumstance whatsoever will you ever have warm water (Cuba, Honduras, Guatemala to name a few). Some showers have strings to pull. Some showers have no showerhead at all, just a gravitating flow of water. We like to refer to these as enema showers...For apparent reasons. I have encountered several of these in the States as well. A certain Motel 6 in the San Francisco Bay area comes to mind.

I can still vividly recall shivering in a damp, rank, Berlin flophouse run by a mustachioed Russian woman with a bad attitude. That particular shower was a curtain less affair without a reservoir to retain the water, thus it ran out into the bathroom and eventually out into the room itself. The fun never ends!

Manga, Manga

Italy, 1997

Manga, manga, or eat, eat, is normally not a phrase associated with fear or anxiety. Unless of course you find yourself sitting at a dinner table in the Italian countryside dining on hairy pigskin and drinking some really nasty homemade wine.

While journeying through Europe with my friend, Dusty Decarlo, we had the opportunity to experience some rural living in an Italian town called San Giuliano. Dusty had relatives that lived in the city of Campobasso (pop. 50,000) and the town of San Giuliano (pop. 1200). Although they were relatives, Dusty knew them about as well as I did...Or, in other words...Not at all. Tired of big cities, we jumped on the opportunity to visit the small town where Dusty's relatives hailed from. Dusty's dad, a doctor in Ohio, relayed many stories over the years about the fabled little hamlet, so we were eager to see the place for ourselves.

We enjoyed a modern, high-speed train from Rome to Varaino. In Varaino, modern convenience screeched to a halt, and we were transported to a much earlier era. We transferred from the high-speed train to a low-speed train. The train actually resembled a Greyhound Bus from the 1940s. It had two clunky gears and smelled like a steel mill. But, it did bring us to where we needed to go in Campobasso and that was the important thing. Style definitely took a backseat to necessity.

We were met at the train station in Campobasso by Sylvanna and Rafael. They were in their forties, and I guess, would have been

Dusty's distant aunt and uncle or some such thing? They had a daughter named Marie Antoinette, who was in her twenties. She was cute and I crossed my fingers that she would fare better than her namesake.

They transported us through Campobasso in a driving rain and rush hour traffic to San Giuliano, where we met Theresa Decarlo, a grandmotherly-type in her seventies. Grandma lived alone in a grand old house. The house was constructed in 1754. It was authentic as hell. Even had a former stable in the basement.

For that matter, the whole damn town was authentic as hell. Its 1200 residents lived on top of a hill in a medieval city overlooking a foggy valley filled with vineyards and various other crops. The town had changed very little in the past fifty or perhaps, three hundred years. When we went out for a walk, people came outside to take a look at us. We were a real novelty in San Giuliano. Almost celebrities. Too bad there weren't any sweet young groupies.

Grandma didn't speak any English, so I did my best to communicate with her in Spanish, which was close enough to Italian most of the time. She desired to grab and kiss our cheeks, which she did over and over again. Especially me.

The only time I remember seeing her look disappointed, was when I slept in the wrong bed. I awoke to her grieving moans and never did quite understand why she was so upset. Maybe the other bed was bigger or had more blankets on it or something? The covers had no bearing anyway, as I opted to sleep inside my sleeping bag instead of beneath the leaden, circa 1912, claustrophobic, x-ray-certified top cover.

Dinner time. The pork chops roasted along nicely in the fireplace on a little grill. They probably would have been really tasty, had they been cooked. I don't know about you, but I don't savvy raw pork. Grandma pulled the chops off the grill and placed them in front of us... Blood dripping down on the plate. I tried my best to explain to her the seriousness involved in eating raw pork, but she would have none of that. She just grabbed my cheeks and emphatically moaned "manga, manga" over and over. She looked like she might even cry if we didn't dig in. We poked around them and somehow managed not to get sick. Just when we thought we might escape the dinner table, the pasta arrived. A heaping bowl of the homemade, hand-rolled, variety. More than I can eat in a week. Next, a full salad with bread, followed by sliced apples, along with a very tart, white wine. Somehow we survived the assault and enjoyed our quiet evening in the country watching hilarious Italian television programming.

The next morning we went out for a walk in the valley below (managing to get lost only once). Before leaving, we caught a glimpse of some pigskin, complete with tiny hairs, boiling on the stove. I told Dusty it was our night's dinner and he laughed loudly. Little did he know.

After watching modern-looking women carry baskets on their heads and medieval-looking women harvest walnuts (dressed in 1503 era garb, hoods included) in the rain, we stopped off at the town bar and sampled some of the local flavor. It wasn't that good. But, nobody ever said Italy was renowned for its beer anyway.

As we arrived back at the house for dinner, Sylvanna, Rafael, Marie Antoinette, and Rafael's mother (name?) joined us. Sure enough, pigskins all around. Along with sausage nuggets, apples, salad, pasta, and some of Rafael's homemade wine (sorry, but it was really bad as well). As soon as Grandma turned her back after placing the skins on my plate, I flicked them on Dusty's plate with my fork. Something he would have done, I might add. The disgusted look on his face was classic. He never actually ate the fried cilia skins. He just moved them around on his plate.

Later on in the evening, we went out with Marie Antoinette and her boyfriend Georgio. Marie Antoinette's communist friend Sylvia accompanied as well.

We discussed the political ramifications of Sylvia's desire to form a communist-Italian state while eating pizza in a local bar. She was a member of the local communist party and several of her party's candidates had already taken office. She was enthused. I guess they weren't watching Russia's woes in the final stages of communism. Or, they were too busy watching the new, struggling Russian system too closely. I don't know which.

I couldn't take my eyes off Georgio. And it wasn't because he was a handsome man that turned me on, but because he was a dead ringer for Dusty's dad as a younger man. It was simply uncanny. Then I started looking around and I saw Dusty's dad everywhere I looked. They all had "the look". I was totally blown away...Speechless. I often wonder how Grandma and the gang are doing. Damn bunch of Reds.

Andrea and the Pipeline

Alaska, 1997

As Dusty Decarlo and I drove through
Fairbanks, we somehow came up with a hair-
brained scheme to drive to Prudhoe Bay on the
north coast of Alaska. Even though oil
production and transportation dominate the area,
we seemed to fancy the notion of camping out on
the beach beside the Arctic Ocean. I don't know
what the hell we actually expected the place to
look like, but we were determined...And we had
time on our hands. Neither of us had jobs or
wives to get home to at the time. So in other
words, it really didn't matter where we drove
to.

Leaving Fairbanks and North Pole, Alaska (a
real place by the way), we jumped on the Dalton
Highway, which would, hypothetically anyway,
take us all the way to the town of Deadhorse and
Prudhoe Bay. Deadhorse is approximately 500
miles from Fairbanks. Of those 500 miles, 440
of them are dirt...Or more specifically...Mud.
A dirt racetrack for oversized semis and
pipeline maintenance crews, as the Trans Alaska
Pipeline follows the Dalton Highway. Or I
should say, the Dalton Highway follows the
pipeline.

There are no *Circle K's*, *Safeways*,
McDonalds, or billboards...In all honesty,
there's nothing at all for the first 120 miles.
Just empty space until you reach the Yukon
River, where you better gas up and buy whatever
supplies you need...If you can.

The Dalton Highway is by no means comparable
to I-90 or any other Interstate in the U.S. It
is definitely dissimilar to a leisurely drive
from Tucson to Los Angeles down I-10.

For the first 120 miles, we crept up and down ravines, through stunted, dwarf-like pine trees that resembled pipe cleaners. It was autumn, and blazing oranges, reds, and yellows colored the landscape. We eventually reached the Yukon River at around 6 p.m.

The settlement at the Yukon River consisted of a gas station and garage, a small restaurant, and some storage facilities for boats. As sparse as it was, it was like entering Chicago in relation to the emptiness preceding it.

We pulled in at the gas station and were met by a woman resembling the late Chris Farley. She had fiery-red hair and a very rotund physique. She appeared very happy to see us...Probably happy to see anybody. She asked us if we wanted to drink a beer and smoke a real tasty cigar. Seeing as though we were in no hurry, we obliged. She turned and started walking into the garage and I asked her where I should park my truck? "Where it's at is all right with me", she replied. I was taken aback for a second, then laughed, remembering I was in the middle of nowhere and not at a Chevron Station in Phoenix. I moved my truck anyway.

After introductions, we followed Andrea up a set of stairs in the garage area to an apartment that overlooked the gas pumps. She told us that the owners were presently away at "some sort of cult meeting" in Fairbanks. Even the kids.

Andrea's apartment was a real dump, complete with rotting foodstuffs and dirty clothes splayed out all over the floor. She offered us a beer, which we grudgingly accepted. Not because we didn't want one, but because we knew how much beers cost her there in the middle of nowhere. $20 + a twelve-pack. But Andrea insisted. She was just elated to have some company. She said it had been quite awhile since she had any visitors. I could tell it had also been quite awhile since she cleaned her apartment.

I remember looking out the window and down onto the Yukon River and just finding the whole experience unbelievable. Here we were partying with Chris Farley's sister inside a grubby apartment in the gathering dusk in the middle of nowhere, Alaska. With absolutely nobody around.

After awhile, Andrea received a call from a trucker down the road asking if she could change a flat on his semi. "No problem", she replied.

Leaving Andrea to attend to her business, we ventured down to the Yukon River to set up camp for the night. Andrea said she'd meet us down there later on.

The Yukon River is a mammoth river, which chugs its way out of the Richardson Mountains in the Yukon Territory of Canada as the Porcupine River. Turning into the Yukon River it runs all the way through the heart of Alaska and eventually enters the Bering Sea on the West Coast. Since it was autumn, and Moose Season in Alaska, there were hunters in odd, ramshackle crafts plying the river in search of prey. Some of the boats were small bass fishing type boats, while others were huge dilapidated houseboats.

We had another use in mind for the Yukon River...Baths...We took a bath every four or five days whether we needed it or not...We usually needed it. Several of our outdoor bathtubs on the trip included icy-cold glacier streams, which displayed a chalky white color. These particular baths tended to cause immediate ice-cream-headaches as you stuck your head under the freezing current. But you sure felt refreshed afterward!

Andrea appeared after an hour or so, armed with more beer, and accompanied by three dogs, two of which had only three legs. Apparently the unfortunate dogs wandered into traps. As we sat talking in lawn chairs around the fire in complete darkness, a boat absent of any light source whatsoever, suddenly came racing down the river and up onto the bank next to us. The crazy son of a bitch jumped out of the boat with a smile screwed on his face and joined us for a beer. After a few hours, we bid Andrea farewell, thanking her for all her hospitality. Being as lonely as she was, I was a bit afraid she was going to try and molest us...But thankfully...She didn't.

The following morning we awoke to rain and very low visibility. We ventured slowly up the Dalton Highway toward Deadhorse through thick mud. All sorts of strange looking oilrig equipment passed by us on the road. Some of the contraptions looked like maybe they were more suited for Mars than the tundra of Alaska. There were even trailer homes situated on tank tracks that apparently roamed across the vast permafrost. One handsome woman in particular, jumped out of a pickup with a friendly warning for us..."An eleven-foot wide lowboy is coming down the road right behind me, so watch your damn ass". We did.

Eventually, we passed a few noncommercial vehicles heading back toward Fairbanks with mud caked all the way up to their windows. A Volkswagen Bus puttered by, sliding all over the road. We couldn't imagine what they were thinking. If you didn't have four-wheel drive on that messy road, you were in deep shit...Literally.

We reached the Arctic Circle (there's actually a sign that signifies your arrival) and had soup and crackers on the tailgate in honor of the achievement. Signs inform travelers of the -80 degree Fahrenheit temperatures in the winter months and the extreme temperature swings from day to night. The climate is very similar to the southwestern deserts in that respect. It can be 72 degrees at my house in Phoenix during the day and then cool down to the high 20s at night. You learn to dress in layers.

As the skies lightened and the sun appeared, we donned short-sleeved t-shirts. That night, we sat around the fire wearing winter jackets. Extreme swings for sure. In the winter above the Arctic Circle, you can actually throw a bucket of water out the door and watch it turn to ice before it hits the ground. Now that's cold.

Inching forward down the slick road, we made it to the town of Coldfoot. Coldfoot is 120 miles from Andrea and the Yukon River and a "mere" 250 miles from our destination on the Arctic Ocean. It's also the last place to gas up. And you pay the price...Like it or not.

Coldfoot consists of a gas station, a cafe, rusting cars, and several crummy buildings. Coldfoot also boasted a pay phone, which I utilized to converse with several friends working their asses off in the Lower 48. I just had to rub it in.

We camped forty miles north of Coldfoot that night within sight of the beautiful Brooks Range and the Gates of the Arctic. We kicked up some moose while hiking around on the tors or craggy hills in the area and jumped up and down on the spongy, surreal-feeling permafrost.

The next morning, we were met by wet snow showers as we attempted once more to traverse the muddy road. After several hours of sliding on and off the road, and into the ditch a few times, we decided to abandon our goal to get to Deadhorse.

We were pretty bummed, but it was definitely the smart thing to do at the time. If you break an axle or slide down into a steep canyon up there...You're screwed...Period. We also heard from Andrea and several others at the cafe in Coldfoot, that there really is no public access to Prudhoe Bay. The only way to actually venture out to the ocean is through a chartered trip by the oil companies for $25. I guess our plan to camp along the shores of the Arctic Ocean was pretty goofy to begin with. But it sure as hell sounded good didn't it?

Ghosts of the Galiuros

Arizona, 1997

Sometimes you just have to get away all by yourself in order to evaluate and reassess your life. This seems to be the case all too often for me. Or perhaps, I go away all by myself because nobody else wants to go with me? Either way, this story centers on a solo-backpacking trip to the Galiuro Mountains in southeastern Arizona.

I wasn't completely solo, as I was accompanied by my faithful Golden Retriever, Quinnie. And no, I'm not vain enough to name my dog after myself; she was actually named by an ex-girlfriend. Therefore, I'm bound by the silly name.

The main reason for my trip to the Galiuro Wilderness was to investigate the Power's cabin located on Rattlesnake Creek. The site bore witness to a brutal shootout on February 10th, 1918. Having read detailed accounts on the event, I had always wanted to check the place out for myself. And besides, the surrounding area is beautiful. The Galiuro Wilderness is really more like a mountain island, with desert encircling the small mountain range.

The cabin was owned by Thomas Jefferson Power. On that fateful February morning, the cabin was occupied by old man Power, his two sons, Tom and John, and a family friend and ex-army scout, Tom Sisson. The occupants of the cabin were awakened by the jangling sounds of their mare's bell at dawn, causing old Jeff Power to believe a mountain lion was prowling around outside. A common occurrence. Grabbing his .30/.30 Winchester, Jeff Power opened the front door and was immediately immersed in a hail of gunfire.

Four "lawmen" consisting of T.K. Wootan, Frank McBride, Frank Haynes, and Martin R. Kempton had come to the cabin at dawn to deliver warrants to Tom and John Power for draft evasion. The Power brothers were reportedly "slackers", a term coined in that era that applied to "draft dodgers" (another coined phrase).

Although there is plenty of controversy surrounding the basis for the warrants and the underlying reasons behind the lawmen's timing in serving them, *one thing is certain*; the gun battle became fast and furious and left old Jeff Power, McBride, Kempton, and Wootan dead on the frosty ground.

Tom and John Power each incurred permanent damage to their left eyes as a result of flying glass and splinters.

After the brief, but deadly gun battle, Frank Haynes rode off toward the town of Klondyke for reinforcements, while Tom Sisson (who claimed to have hid under the bed during the entire firefight and therefore witnessed nothing), along with the injured Power brothers fled the scene. The trio knew a posse would soon be organized and hot on their trail.

The event triggered the largest manhunt in Arizona history, as 3,000 men on horseback and automobile scoured the countryside, through rugged terrain for nearly a month before finally capturing the trio. The men were sentenced to prison and the Power brothers served 42 years (still the longest time served in an Arizona prison to date), while Sisson died behind bars.

There is some speculation even today, that the real, underlying reason behind the shootout was a monetary one...That Wootan wanted the Power gold mine, which had recently received new equipment and was ready to convert its rich ore contents. In any event, I was very intrigued by the story and wanted to see the location of the shootout for myself.

I struck out from Phoenix in my four-wheel-drive Nissan and traversed through congested freeways past several accidents and construction delays before finally obtaining some measure of breathing space near Florence Junction on Highway 60. After pumping gas and eating burned Egg Mcmuffins in Globe, I continued eastward on Route 70.

As I was about to turn south onto Klondyke Road and the Galiuros, I spotted a little store on the side of the road in which to purchase a few large cans of beer for the trip and stopped. I had to wait in line while several Native Americans from the Apache Reservation stocked up on supplies...Namely, caseloads of Budweiser and bottles of Jim Beam. The fact that it was nine in the morning apparently bore little weight to their decisions and they soon attracted several other tribal members to the counter in admiration of their purchases. Asking if maybe he could tag along, a gentleman possessing a single tooth exclaimed, "If I'd a known you guys was doin' a run, I wouldn't have come all the way down here myself, why didn't you tell me". I guess I can't really talk...I was there for beer at 9:00 a.m. as well.

A word here about the Apaches. I don't want to sound like I'm slamming the tribe, but sometimes I feel like somebody has to.

I wholeheartedly respect the ways of the Native American of the past. I have filled countless hours enthralled in reading and investigating Indians of the past. I, like many Midwestern boys, grew up romanticizing the Indian way of life, and often took on the role as an Indian when playing cowboys and Indians. I cheered as I read of the many triumphs of Cochise, Geronimo, Plenty-Coup, and Black Hawk to list a few. I believe the Indians received a raw deal...No two ways about it. On the other hand, give me an example of a defeated group of people anywhere throughout history that hasn't received a raw deal. Unfortunately, the spoils go to the victors. Sad...But reality.

The state of affairs today on the reservation is simply tragic. Casinos or not. It is almost impossible to explain the situation to someone living in New York or Chicago, as they hold fast to their childhood images, or those obtained through television. The only way to really have an opinion is to witness reservation life for yourself. But if you can't...Here's an update: tarpaper shacks with peeling, fading, pink and lime green paint, mounds of garbage (some of it smoldering in piles near the road), packs of wild dogs roaming here, there, and nowhere in particular, roadside jewelry sales, perplexed pickup trucks, rotting refrigerators, rusty bedsprings, littered beer cans, satellite dishes and lots of bottles, most of them broken. It's not a pretty sight.

Some of you might think I'm being mean or callous, but I'm actually rooting hard for them to turn it around. If not for themselves, then for the environment.

And if you really want to see the damage alcohol has caused the Native American, go ahead and spend a Saturday night drinking Garden Deluxe (cheap grain alcohol) in a bar in Gallup, New Mexico. Just try not to run anyone over on I-40 as you leave town, as someone is always wont to cross that stretch of foggy, icy road directly in front of you in the predawn hours.

All right, I think I've done enough soap boxing, so I'll get back to the trip.

I eventually managed buy my two cans of beer and to traverse the dirt roads leading to the trailhead, passing by beautiful Aravaipa Canyon on the way.

Throwing my pack on, I headed up the steep, rugged trail full of loose boulders. The landscape included scrub junipers, prickly pear cacti, century plants, and a host of colorful wildflowers. Huge spires and odd-shaped rock formations loomed above me as I hiked onward, stopping periodically to take on water. I eventually came across a series of creeks, where Quinnie found relief from the heat, by wallowing around in the cool water and red mud.

In the late afternoon hours, I began contemplating a campsite for the night. Unfortunately, the plateau that I was traversing, offered little in the way of water, so I pressed on. I wound my way around several jagged cliffs and craggy ravines before descending down into what I believed was the Power Garden and Ranch according to my map. The trail became very steep and loose rocks and boulders caused me to lose my footing on multiple occasions. I have to admit I was a bit nervous on the way down, simply because it was getting dark and had I broken my ankle...I would have been in serious trouble, as I hadn't seen anyone on the trail all day...Which wasn't a bad thing, mind you.

I dropped down into Horse Canyon, which treated me to a carpet of dead leaves to walk on and luxurious pines, oaks, cottonwoods, and alligator junipers to walk beneath. I stopped to filter water from a pool in the creek and then resumed my march down the trail toward the Power cabin. The creek I was following dropped gently down to Rattlesnake Creek, leaving a series of pools and small waterfalls in its wake.

I stopped about a 1/4-mile short of the Power cabin and dropped my pack on the ground.

Continuing pack-free up the trail through a beautiful meadow, which paralleled Rattlesnake Creek, I kept a wary eye out for the creek's namesake slitherers. I soon spotted the cabin and some outlying buildings across the meadow. Even though I hadn't seen anyone all day, I knew that I was following a herd of horses, probably an outfitter and paying dudes, or customers, which left their remains (road apples and *Smarties* wrappers) for me on the trail. Therefore, I wasn't surprised to find a dozen horses grazing within the fenced meadow.

I began to walk up to the cabin, then reconsidered, deciding that I really wasn't in the mood for conversation. It was after all a solo trip. So, I retreated back down the trail to the woods and my pack, where I enjoyed dinner and a beer around the campfire while reading about the Power incident.

It was a beautiful night in the wilderness

beneath a canopy of branches. I slept on the ground under a sterling, full moon. Solitude and peace. It was just too good to be true.

Unfortunately, my peace and solitude were rudely shattered by gunfire in the direction of the Power cabin. I thought maybe the "wranglers" were recreating the shootout for their "dudes", or perhaps they didn't even know the story? Either way, there was some sort of mayhem and they continued yelling like idiots long into the night.

A word about outfitting. I know...I already railed on the Apaches and now I'm jumping right back on that proverbial soapbox again. But this will be the last time...I promise.

Personally, I have nothing against outfitters trying to make a buck, while utilizing the National Forests and Wilderness areas...Well maybe just a little, but that's beside the point.

Having come into contact with outfitters and their dudes on several trips in Arizona and Wyoming, I have grown to resent both the attitude and the trash left behind by them. It appears to me that the outfitters feel it is their birthright to establish themselves as the lords of the land. I sometimes think feel they believe they are the sole reason for the trail's existence in the first place.

In Wyoming a few years back, I was on a backpacking trip in the Bridger-Teton Wilderness with my good friend John "Javelina Sours" Sweet and came upon two "pack trains" along the trail. In each instance, there was a trail of wrappers and cans littered behind along with condescending attitudes from the riders as they passed by.

Why? I have no idea? I guess it would have been too much trouble to be friendly, or to get down off the damned horses and pick up their trash. I realize that many of these "city slickers" would never have the chance to experience the wilderness any other way, but shit, have a little respect for the land. Sorry...I just had to say something.

I rolled over in my sleeping bag the next morning and came face to face with a wild turkey. My dog was so beat and tired, she never even jumped up and attacked the old tom. He was a huge specimen. After eating breakfast and filling my canteens, I ventured down to the cabin, dudes or no dudes.

Happily, I found the place deserted. On closer inspection, I discovered that the bureaucrats in Washington had declared the buildings as "Administrative Sites" at the ranch. For what reason or purpose...It was beyond me? I came to the conclusion that the Feds were probably in cahoots with the outfitters and probably made some extra cash on the side by renting out the "Administrative Sites". Sorry for my mistrustful attitude.

After spending the morning checking out the site, I started down Rattlesnake Creek and made my way to the southern loop, which would take me back out of the wilderness to my truck, via a different route. The creek ran intermittently. And the trail at times, was less than intermittent, and sometimes downright nonexistent. The trail became invisible altogether as I approached Corral Spring (about two miles from Rattlesnake Creek). Filling my canteens again, I searched in vain for the trail and then decided to climb a steep precipice that was home to several waterfalls.

Although very picturesque, the canyon was narrow and vertically inclined, and all but impossible for Quinnie to climb up. She did her best to jump up and to claw with her nails at the cliff face, but most of the time, she slid back down and I had to push or pull her up.

We eventually regained the trail and hiked a series of switchbacks to the Kennedy Peak Saddle, where I had originally planned on camping for the night. The 360-degree views were spectacular, but unfortunately water was very scarce, so I began to hike down the trail toward the truck in hopes of finding a suitable spot somewhere down lower.

Unable to find water at all, I ended up

hiking the rest of the way down to the truck as lusty visions of *Whoppers* danced merrily through my head. The backup plan was to camp at the truck, where I had plenty of water. The problem now was wood and there was none to be had on the rolling, barren plain where my truck was parked.

So, the *Whopper* in my head won out and I packed up and headed for Globe. The three-day hike was squeezed into two because of the water situation, but I was satisfied nevertheless.

I must have anticipated the long-awaited *Whopper* in my mind a bit too much however, as it didn't taste very good after all the buildup.

Quinnie and I found a dirt road above the copper clouds and city lights of Miami, Arizona and tiredly reminisced about the past day's events. Watching the full moon pass over us; we quietly fell asleep.

Russian Marriage Agency

Russia, 2001

You feel you're getting up in years and its time that you considered getting hitched. But all your relationships with American women, just haven't seemed to work out. You've heard all about beautiful Russian brides that can't wait to be your wife. Gorgeous, young, enticing, foreign women clambering to come to America and be at your side. Fact or fantasy...Well, maybe a little of both.

Virtually everyone has a friend, acquaintance, or co-worker that either has a foreign bride or they know someone that does...Or used to anyway. I'm not trying to sway anyone's opinion one way or the other with this little vignette, but here's my experience with a Russian marriage agency in St. Petersburg.

About eight months prior to traveling to Russia, Dusty Decarlo and I joked about meeting beautiful Russian women. For kicks, we would get on the Internet and click on various websites that advertised brides-to-be from all over the former Soviet Union. Funny thing was, the same women would appear on multiple websites. We even e-mailed several of the "pictured ladies" and received a few sparse responses in return. We came to the conclusion that most of the websites were basically scams...Just our opinion, so don't get pissed off at me if the process worked for you. We merely wanted to meet the women and really didn't have any immediate plans for marriage. Mainly just someone to show us around Moscow, St. Petersburg, and Kiev while traveling through.

As the Russia trip approached, the scenario changed drastically...At least for me anyway, as I became engaged and, meeting beautiful Russians was definitely out of the question. However, Dusty was still single, so a visit to a marriage agency to meet someone who might show us around wasn't completely out of the question.

While waiting in line to see Lenin's corpse in Red Square, an American in front of us turned around and proudly introduced his "new" wife to us. After contacting an agency, he had corresponded with the young woman for several months, prior to making the journey to meet her in Moscow. Contrary to what some people think, the process is rather lengthy, and by no means a "quickie" in the legal sense. Paperwork has to be filed, cards have to be issued...The whole nine yards before the blushing bride arrives in the United States to keep you warm.

A brief word on Lenin. There remains controversy as to whether the corpse residing in the mausoleum, is actually Lenin, or a convincing imposter. To be honest, it was very hard to tell. Then again, I didn't really have the chance to hang out with the man when he was alive, so my ability to judge his likeness is severely impaired. No cameras are allowed inside the building and tourists are ushered around his body, which lay in state, at a fast clip. Any dawdling is quickly rectified by a prodding guard's machine gun. Either way, it's all pretty damned spooky and macabre.

Back to the brides. In Moscow, we met at least a dozen foreign men, most American, in the process of getting to know their new wives to be. The pattern was fairly standard. Middle-aged men with some cash and young attractive women without any. Most of the women have kids and are looking for a way to raise and support them. The men, well you know what they're looking for. On the surface anyway, it appears to be a win-win situation.

As far as the claims of beautiful women in Russia. Believe them...They're true. I've been all over the world and I can vouch for the fact

that Russia is right up there in the top echelon
when it comes to beauty. As for personality and
other attributes, I don't know.
But I don't think most of the guys we met were
all that interested in the women's personalities
anyway. Just my humble assumption. I think
they had other things on their mind.

After touring Moscow, we headed by train to
St. Petersburg. While reading an English
language newspaper in St. Petersburg, I came
across various ads for "marriage agencies". I
tried to convince Dusty to go to one of them,
just to see what they were all about. I was
curious. He was too, but perhaps a bit
apprehensive as well. Finally he agreed to go
to one if I could find the place (He really
didn't think I would). No small task in St.
Petersburg. I don't know any Russian and the
street signs alone can wreak havoc on your mind.

Just about the time we had forgotten all
about the silly marriage agency scheme, we ran
right into the place he had challenged me to
locate.

While resting against a wall on Nevsky
Prospekt, the main drag in St. Pete, I looked up
and noticed a side street that appeared to be
the same name as in the ad. Sure enough, right
down the block, we found the Fortuna Marriage
Agency. However, now that I had actually found
the place, Dusty didn't want to go in. It took
a little convincing, but after a few minutes of
negotiation, we walked inside to investigate the
scene.

A courteous, but very serious woman appeared
to greet us at the door. We could tell right
away that this was very serious business to
them. We did our best to retain straight faces
and took a seat in a little room. Another woman
came in and asked us what we had in mind. Dusty
rattled off an age continuum and she disappeared
into a storeroom, emerging a few seconds later
with a stack of binders filled with pictures and
profiles. When I say stack, I mean a huge stack
about four feet high off the ground. And those
were just the women in the age bracket between

24 and 32.

The woman left us alone to peruse the stack. She gave Dusty a pen and paper to write down the names of the women he wanted to meet. We sat there in complete disbelief at the pile of three-ring binders on the table in front of us. I took a few snapshots which probably didn't go over to well with the staff...But what the hell, it really was comical seeing Dusty surrounded with thousands of glossy women on the coffee table in front of him.

We each took a stack and spent the next hour or so checking out Russian women. Dusty picked out four or five from the thousand or so pictures. We had to constantly rework the women's ages, as the profiles were dated and some of the women listed as 24 years-old, were now 28 or 29 years-old.

The agency attendant returned and took down the names of the women that Dusty had chosen from the stack. She said that it would $5 USD for a phone number and $15 USD for a meeting at the agency. Dusty opted for the meeting at the agency.

The attendant called the first couple of numbers and found that the women were no longer interested or were missing in action. We were told to search the rolls again. Eventually, she managed to schedule two meetings, back to back, the following day. Dusty gave her $30 USD and we left with a big smile on our faces. The whole deal was hysterical.

Dusty insisted I back him up the next day in his meetings with the Russian beauties. We sat on a couch and awaited the arrival of contestant number one. The woman, a pretty blonde nurse, arrived and immediately had a problem with my presence. She didn't know why I was there, but she made it very clear she wanted me to leave. So I left and walked around St. Petersburg during their three-hour meeting.

Since the meetings were back to back, I actually walked around for six hours and met back up with Dusty in the late afternoon. He was accompanied by contestant number two...Olga.

Olga was a well-endowed, 27 year-old brunette fashion designer. She had actually joined the stable at the agency on a dare by her friends several months earlier. She joined us for dinner and then continued to show us all around her city for several days after. So you see, we accomplished the task of finding a beautiful tour guide after all. As for marriage...Probably not. As for lasting friendship...Definitely. Dusty has remained in touch over the past few years with Olga and her friends. He has traveled to St. Petersburg three times since our first encounter. Renting out an apartment and continuing his search for whatever he's searching for?

So what's the bottom line here? I don't know. But one thing is certain...There really are beautiful ladies in Russia. And if you want to bring one home...Have at it...They're waiting for you.

Childhood Lessons

Arizona, 2003

As we approach adulthood, we dismiss some of the many lessons from our childhood days. Some may be far to basic, some outdated and some we may have forgotten altogether. However, there are several critical childhood lessons that have strongly applied to my travels abroad.

Everybody remembers the familiar warning to look both ways when crossing the street. As an adult, the process is nearly automatic, a reflex action. Simply a survival skill. If you fail to look both directions when crossing the street you might die, simple as that.

So there I am in Kuala Lumpur, Malaysia crossing a busy street. Well...Maybe it was a freeway and I probably shouldn't have been crossing it anyway, but there weren't any bridges and I wasn't going to walk three miles out of my way. I looked both ways and scooted across to the median separating the eight-lane freeway. Looking right, I saw that everything looked clear, so I took a step off the median and prepared to run across. At that very moment, or microsecond, I instinctively looked left and noticed the maelstrom of cars bearing down on me. I reflexively leaped backwards to the safety of the median, thanking my parents for drilling the concept into my head.

The act itself seemed so trivial...Crossing the street. However, throw in the fact that Malaysians drive on the opposite side of the road (left like Brits) and your brain begins to wobble at times. Everything is backwards. Even mundane chores like walking down the sidewalk in a crowd. As an American, I think right sided. Stay to the right, the flow is right. In London or Malaysia however, the flow is left. Sure, you can be cool, or stupid, and buck the system, but going against the grain can be costly and really piss someone off if you run into them. Test it out for yourself by walking the left side at a football game and watch as people give you dirty looks or throw things at you. We're programmed...Pure and simple.

I'll never forget renting a car in Dublin, Ireland. After picking up our luggage, we threw it in the trunk and prepared to leave the parking lot. Problem was, I jumped into the wrong seat. After rectifying the situation, I ambled down the road, trying to overcome the overwhelming feeling that I was doing something heinous or wrong...Like driving on the wrong side of the road.

Everything is opposite. Even the controls. You shift with your left hand. Not that big a deal, just a mind wrapper, that's all. I can't tell you how many times during the ten-day journey through Ireland that I found myself leaving a parking lot on the wrong side of the road. Or for that matter how many times I left a restaurant and opened the passenger door and prepared to drive. It sounds asinine, but our minds do really work in patterns. As if narrow roads, roundabouts, and sheep all over the bloody road weren't enough to contend with!

The childhood phrase "watch what you eat" definitely comes into play when traveling abroad. The meaning of the phrase may be tweaked a little though, as it's not weight gain or nightmares one worries about, but sickness. I'm all for trying exotic dishes and broadening my horizons, but there are limits to be sure. For instance, I stay away from street vendors. Oh, the food smells great, and it may even taste heavenly, but the aftereffects are tragic at times. Could even ruin your whole trip. I'll leave the goat eyes for someone else.

There are a few childhood phrases that sort of become silly as an adult. For instance the phrase "don't talk to strangers" is a hard promise to keep in a place where everyone is a stranger. Besides, what fun would that be?

That's how you really learn about a culture.

And what about receiving gifts from strangers. I don't think any of the third world kids ever heard of that one. They always want something from a stranger, namely candy and pens...And sometimes your wallet.

Even the Saturday night bath routine comes into play. I always try to bathe once a week while on the road, whether I need it or not. I just wish others on the road would follow suit. I recall a European girl named Mirta, who needed a few lessons on hygiene. She damn near stunk us out of our hotel room in Guatemala when we let her travel with us for a few days. Perhaps however in her case, it was more closely linked to the concept of watching what you eat?

Hangin' Out with Maximon

Guatemala/Honduras 2002

If you're into ancient ruins, volcanoes, rainforests, and chicken buses, then Guatemala's the place for you. I had always been fascinated by pictures of Tikal, in northeastern Guatemala, with its amazing Mayan temples rising out of the stubborn jungle floor. Curious toucans, parrots, and howler monkeys unleashing their cries into the thick air. A subtle threat of danger and the unknown.

I managed to somehow talk my old traveling companions Dusty Decarlo and Christian Bates into going with me. It's always hard to find friends that are willing to travel to third world countries on a miniscule budget. Willing and able to forego the pleasures of fancy hotels and room service for the opportunity to absorb the culture whilst living among the average citizen.

When it comes right down to it, there are very few people I know that are willing to travel as shoddily as I do. Part of the reason I travel as I do is the fact that I'm basically a poor bastard. Aside from that blatant fact, I really enjoy seeing a country from its roots up. I don't personally have anything against the Hyatt Regency or Embassy Suites, I simply can't afford them and I don't particularly care to hang out with a bunch of tourists while on holiday. I see enough of them at home.

However, that last statement is a bit misleading, as I tend not to come across a whole hell of a lot of Yanks on my travels abroad. They tend to stay closer to home. Disneyland, Sea World, the Daytona 500...

We flew into Guatemala City and quickly caught a cab to Antigua, which lies about an hour outside the capital. In fact, Antigua was itself the capital prior to 1773, when a large earthquake rocked the city and prompted officials to relocate the capital in 1776 to its present location in Guatemala City. Quakes, by the way, also rock Guatemala City.

Antigua attracts many tourists to its cobbled, stone streets and Spanish colonial architecture. Antigua truly is Central America's crown jewel city. Three volcanoes ring the city, offering orange, lava-flow displays in the evening, which we observed gloriously from the roof of our flophouse.

There are plenty of Indian markets, parades, and performances to keep a guy busy for a few days. You can also hike up the volcanoes if you so choose. Just be careful, as occasionally hikers are pummeled by pumice.

We were privy to colorful fireworks and a sensationally clean and florally decked out town in anticipation of the Pope's visit.

After a few days in Antigua we hopped on a rickety bus to Honduras to investigate the ruins at Copan. Riding a bus in Guatemala is a rather hair-raising experience. Who needs a thrilling bungee jump when you can ride a chicken bus? To our dismay, we actually missed out on the chicken bus experience. Not that the buses we rode on were much better, they just didn't have any livestock strapped to the roof.

Chicken buses are "retired" American and Canadian school buses which are driven down the Pan-American Highway and repainted in wild colors and designs. They rumble down the winding, narrow highways extremely overburdened and an attendant actually stands in the doorway, pulling patrons and their belongings into the bus as it slows down. The buses seldom stop completely.

We were witness to a chicken bus that took a corner a little too hot and actually rode along on three wheels for an instant or so. Scary stuff believe you me.

The bus left Antigua at 4 a.m. and treated us to all kinds of bizarre sights on the way to Honduras. Banana and coconut trees whirred by the windows outside and it appeared to me that there was absolutely no level ground to be found in Guatemala. Corn was growing on 70% grades! I have no idea how they harvested the stuff? Maybe with ropes and harnesses?

Arriving in Copan, Honduras, we spent the afternoon riding some beat horses out into the woods, where we checked out some minor ruins and Dusty and Christian got cozy with a possum, or some such similar rat that was hanging out in a tree. Our guide had designs on eating the furry little critter, but he changed his mind (at least until we were out of sight), deciding instead to keep him as a pet.

The area around Copan is reminiscent (to me anyway) of Ohio in July. Hot, humid, very green, yet not full-on jungle. Lots of coffee and corn growing everywhere along the Copan River. There were also plenty of posters in town warning visitors to watch themselves around Ruby Lake, where several women had been raped and murdered. Their hands cut off by machetes. Everyone in Copan wore a machete on his side, so I guess it was hard to find the culprit?

We hadn't planned on visiting Ruby Lake anyway, but there was always the threat of terrorism, or more likely, robbery when traveling by bus through the jungles of El Peten, where robberies are common. Generally speaking, there is always the risk of being robbed while traveling. As a foreigner, and especially an American, there is a broad assumption of wealth. "All Americans are rich".

That night we played around in the rain, as thunderstorms rolled in one after the next, drenching the little town of Copan Ruinas. Dusty took time out to wash his clothes on the roof of our hotel. Unfortunately his sandals paid the price during the deluge. Crossing the street he stepped through a puddle and for the duration of the trip his sandals "smelled like old ass", according to Dusty. It took two months at the bottom of his pool in Florida to rid the heinous odor.

Christian enjoyed monkey on a stick from a

street vendor, which Dusty and I are always happy to buy for him, knowing one day his luck will run dry and his iron gut will give way to the gurgles. I think they actually did on this particular trip, but he says his bowel troubles were the result of the anti-malarial pills we were taking. I think it was the monkey.

We dined on pork chops w/pineapple, fried bananas, rice, beans and beer at an open-air restaurant in between rounds of thunderstorms. After dinner we walked around the small, hilly town in the pouring rain, soaked to the bone.

The next morning we walked down to the Copan ruins, which are probably the most impressive ruins in Honduras. The complex was occupied by 20,000 Mayans at its peak and the area around Copan shows evidence of being populated since 1200 BC or earlier. The Olmec influence in the region has been dated by their gravesites to 900-600 BC. Copan boasts a ball court, an acropolis, several large plazas, a hieroglyphic stairway, altars, tunnels, and a graveyard.

Perhaps the most striking aspect of Copan are the carved stelae, which are very complete and insanely intricate. Each stela, which is a carved slab of stone, portrays the various rulers of Copan and their accomplishments. The stelae originally had vaults beneath them and a sacrificial altar set up beside them. The stelae portray the reigns of King Smoke Imix (jaguar), King Rabbit, King Smoke Shell, and King Smoke Monkey, to name a few.

We worked up a mighty appetite traipsing through the ruins, so we walked back to town in search of food. We saw a pizza sign and wandered through a gate into what appeared to be someone's back yard. It was and they sold pie. We ordered a supreme pizza, which appeared an hour later decorated with sliced hotdogs and corn. It was pretty bad. But the ambiance was magnificent.

Later that afternoon we caught a bus to the town of Flores on Lake Peten Itza. The charming, grubby little town of Flores is the staging point for trips to the ruins at Tikal.

On the bus we met up with a woman named
Mirta from Holland. She was half-Dutch and
half-Iraqi. She was more than brave (if not a
little naive) traveling through Guatemala by
herself. We agreed to let her tag along with us
for a few days. She was nice, but her hygiene
was a bit lacking as she exuded a hideous body
odor. Even after a shower. Don't ask me?

We survived the long bus ride and
treacherous near-collisions through the
Guatemalan countryside. Somehow we even avoided
being robbed in the pitch-black night. When we
arrived near Flores at 1 a.m., we sat idly on
the bus for a full hour and watched in disbelief
as our bus driver endlessly scarfed down
tortillas and beans. We were incredulous. How
could he sit there eating while we were waiting
to complete the route?

Turns out that we were in fact at the end of
the line and didn't realize it. It's not like
the driver said anything and many of the
passengers were poor campesinos preparing to
sleep on the bus until morning. We finally
figured out what the hell the deal was and hired
a taxi to drive us the rest of the way into the
darkened, shut-down peninsula of Flores at 2
a.m.

The cabbie drove us around town and banged
on doors inquiring into vacancies. There were
none to be had. Finally, as we sat on the curb
preparing to hang out until morning, we found a
hotel room for the exorbitant price of $100 USD.
That doesn't sound like much until you realize
we had been accustomed to paying $5 USD a piece
for a room. We grudgingly paid the price. I
couldn't help but think of Jim Fitzgerald in
Alaska telling us how his budget had been
"fucked all to hell". The next morning we found
a flophouse for $20.

I don't know where to begin in describing
the Mayan ruins at Tikal. Some may remember the
jungle scene at the end of the first *Star Wars*
as the ships flew over the temples and the
treetops. The place is outrageously large. It
was settled by the Maya around 700 BC. The site

is located on a low hill, which gives Tikal some relief from the swampy land and mosquitoes around it. At the time of Christ's birth, the great plaza and temples were taking shape under King Great Jaguar Paw.

The Maya adopted a military tactic from the Aztecs of central Mexico in which they encircled their enemy and launched spears into the crowd. The tactic enabled Tikal to conquer Uaxactun and to reign supreme in the region. At least for awhile anyway. Several hundred years later Lord Water from an area in modern-day southwestern Belize conquered Tikal by ironically using the same spear tactic. The king of Tikal was sacrificed and much of the Peten kingdoms, including Tikal, suffered under Lord Water's rule. At its height, Tikal sprawled over 30 square kilometers and boasted 100,000 inhabitants.

We hiked about eight miles in the rain in order to see the site. And that's only what has been uncovered. There are still plenty of ruins yet concealed by the jungle. Tikal is only rivaled by Chichen Itza, which is located on the Yucatan Peninsula in Mexico, as the greatest Maya site in the Americas.

We hiked through the gigantic archeological playground and climbed the temples. We watched in some degree of horror as other visitors climbed the main temples in strong thunderstorm conditions, lightening crackling all around us. Several climbers even managed to slip on the slick steps and tumble down a ways. Howler monkeys screamed at us from the treetops, while coatimundis scampered close by our sides. It was awesome.

The next day we bid adieu to smelly Mirta and decided to fly back to Guatemala City instead of taking the 12-hour bus ride. It was well worth the $68 for the fifty-minute flight. Mirta opted for a chicken bus. Hope she survived the ride. I also hope the person sitting next to her survived the ride as well.

From Guatemala City we headed back to Antigua for a day then headed northwest to the

town of Panajachel, which is nicknamed
Gringotenango (place of the foreigners). Pana,
as it is known locally, is one of the oldest
tourist hangouts and is located on Lake Atitlan.
There are a lot of gringo hippies around to be
sure. I'm not too hip (no pun intended) on
hanging out with a bunch of tourists (unless
they're really cute of course), but the setting
is what really draws people to Pana. The
bustling little tourist town is located on a
mountainside beside the lake. Three smoking
volcanic peaks; Volcan Toliman (3158m), Volcan
San Pedro (3020m), and Volcan Atitlan (3537m)
tower above the crystal clear, blue lake, which
itself is a caldera, or a collapsed volcanic
cone. The deep lake has a maximum depth of 320
meters.

After finding accommodations, we headed out
on a boat tour of the lake. We crossed the lake
and stopped at several tiny towns, which were in
essence cut off from modern society. The rugged
terrain surrounding the lake prevented travel by
road, thus one had to take a boat to the Pana
side in order to access the highway and enjoy
modern conveniences.

In the town of Santiago Atitlan, we were
assailed by Maximon peddlers while disembarking
from our little boat. They whispered the name
Maximon under their breath as if it were heroin
or hashish they were selling. We had read about
Maximon and were anxious to find him if
possible. As you can see, it wasn't really that
difficult.

Maximon is a highly regarded deity in the
Guatemalan highlands. He also goes by the name
of San Simon and Ry Laj Man. Maximon is a
combination of Mayan gods, Pedro de Alvarado (a
conquistador figure), and the biblical Judas.
Maximon was the Indians response to having
Christian beliefs bestowed on them by the
Spanish. There always has to be somebody
pushing their religion on someone else.

Maximon is a carved wooden statue, clad in
colorful scarves and a sombrero. He also sports
a pair of shades to keep the glare of the

candles off of his eyes. Guatemalans, as well as paying tourists, can make offerings of candles, tobacco, and alcohol to Maximon. A picture costs a few dollars more.

We paid the old salesman and followed him up through steep cobbled roads to a shack where three or four guys kept tabs on Maximon, an honor that is shared amongst town elders and rotates on a yearly basis (I think all of the town elders hang out and drink Maximon's liquor). He clenches a fat cigar between his lips and keeps plenty of rum and tequila shots surrounding his altars. Candles burn brightly throughout the little shack. We were only allowed to look at Maximon for a short while before being shunned away from the holy (or unholy) site. But how about Maximon's keepers? They got it made. All the liquor and tobacco they can handle. After the tourists have left of course. Wouldn't want anyone to think that the sacred offerings were being drank up by a bunch of Maximon entrepreneurs.

The next morning as we left the hotel (surprisingly enough, it was a damn nice one), a kid came running up to me and handed me a t-shirt that I had left behind. I thanked him and grudgingly stuffed the shirt into my pack.

It was my last disposable t-shirt and I had managed to unload several during the trip, lightening my load for trinkets along the way. It was a great system. Less fortunate people acquired t-shirts and I cleaned out my dresser drawers. It was a win-win situation and has become standard procedure for all my travels. I just didn't have the pompous heart to tell the kid I was throwing the shirt away, he wearing rags himself. So I threw it into my bag and I still have the grubby old shirt to this day. Perhaps a few new mortar and grease stains, but it's still intact.

After returning to Antigua through flooded roads, we danced in the streets to festive traditional music, appreciating the culture and volcanic ambiance of Central America. I think I saw Maximon spit out his cigar and smile.

When the Bubble Bursts

Singapore/Malaysia 2002

It's always a horrible feeling to be the last person standing near the conveyor belt at an airport watching miscellaneous cardboard boxes go round and round while your luggage is nowhere to be found.

I landed in Singapore a little after midnight. The airport was completely empty after the passengers on my plane headed out. I left Phoenix at 9 a.m. on Saturday and now it was early Monday morning. Time had literally passed me by. I lost a whole day. I know, I know, I recaptured the lost day when I went home, but nevertheless, the concept never fails to blow me away.

So there I was without my toothbrush half way around the globe, knowing in the back of my mind, that my bag never made the transfer at LAX.

I had to catch a train in the morning to Kuala Lumpur, Malaysia to meet my brother Greg "The Fathead" Quinn, who was there working a golf tournament as a meteorologist.

The baggage office gave me a modest amount of Singapore Dollars and told me they would forward my backpack when it arrived. I took a ride from the only taxi attendant left at the airport to the train station to wait until morning. "Have you heard the news", he asked? The cabbie then proceeded to solemnly relay the details of the bomb blast that rocked an Indonesian nightclub while I was in flight.

I thought the train station would be open all night. I was wrong. I somehow imagined that an ultra-modern city like Singapore must surely have a hospitable train station with all the amenities. At least a restroom and a lounge chair. But when I arrived at 1 a.m., the place was dark...Very dark.

I paid the driver and swung my daypack over my shoulder and circled the train station looking for lights. There weren't any. I did manage to find a few shady characters milling around plastic tables outside the station, drinking beer and smoking bad smelling cigarettes. Thick blue smoke plumes rising up through the dense air.

I figured I might as well see the sights in the city since I had seven hours before my train left. I found a policeman and asked him if it was safe to walk around the city in the wee hours. "No worries", he replied. So, off I went into the muggy, equatorial night to see as many attractions as I possibly could.

Singapore is probably the cleanest large city in the world. Not a strand of refuse anywhere. The locals call it a "fine city", because the authorities fine you for everything from throwing cigarette butts on the sidewalk to chewing bubble gum, which is illegal. Most recall the young American a few years back that went on a graffiti binge. He got the cane. Maybe we ought to break out the cane here in the States. It couldn't hurt.

If I were to offer a nickname for Singapore it would have to be Container City. I have never witnessed so many cargo containers in my life. The docks are full of them. All waiting to be shipped all over the world. Truly a container hub.

After the four-hour walking tour, I went back to the train station and conversed with some of the passengers waiting for the train to Kuala Lumpur. The ethnic mixture in Singapore is chiefly made up of Chinese, Indian, and Malay descent. The Chinese are by far the dominant culture in the city and coincidentally, country of Singapore. In Malaysia, you find the same three backgrounds, but the majority is made up of the Malay descent.

A Malaysian policy called bumiputra, where

the Malay are granted employment positions and slots at universities (a.k.a. affirmative action in reverse), causes some tension and in fact led to race riots in 1969. But overall, the three main races appear to get along fairly well. Although, I must admit I came across very few, if any, interracial couples or children. A phenomenon I inquired about. My assumptions were confirmed as correct.

The Malay control the politics of Malaysia and the Chinese continue to dominate the economic sector. Actually, it's pretty amazing to see such harmony among cultures with such diverse religious beliefs. Muslims, Buddhists, and Hindus all living in close quarters to each other.

The six-hour train ride to Kuala Lumpur gave me a chance to view slash and burn techniques first hand. The rainforest along the tracks is slowly giving way to crops and palm tree farms. There were tiger sightings and even a mauling outside the city of Seremban the day before I blew through on the train. Unfortunately, I saw very little wildlife. Mainly a lot of shacks, shanties, and poverty.

Leaving the city-state of Singapore and entering Malaysia is akin to leaving Tucson and entering Nogales. First world meets third world in the blink of an eye.

Arriving in Kuala Lumpur, I somehow managed to make my way from the train station to my brother's hotel in the suburbs.

As soon as I found out he was working the tournament, a world amateur event, I started scrounging the Internet for tickets. I couldn't resist, having never traveled to Southeast Asia before. Besides, a free hotel room in a foreign land can never be passed up. O.K. sometimes it can. I knew he would be busy most of the time, so this was pretty much a solo excursion. Perhaps a few dinners together throughout the week, in and around his thunderstorm predictions. And the thunderstorms definitely kept him busy. On the other hand, I got to actually enjoy the booming storms.

I snuck in and out of his room at the Hyatt
Regency like a stowaway, making forays into
Kuala Lumpur on the fancy new light rail transit
system, called the LRT. I was careful to be an
equal opportunity explorer, investigating Muslim
mosques, Hindu shrines, and Buddhist temples. I
also made a point to stalk down to Chinatown and
Little India in search of a soccer jersey. If I
ever felt the urge to eat, I just popped into a
market, where chickens roamed free, pigs hung in
effigy and the fish winked at you. I refrained
from eating most of the time. Call me chicken,
but I had too many solo miles to cover and
couldn't afford being sick.

I only managed to get lost a couple times
(attempting shortcuts through the thick woods),
but somehow I made it back to the Hyatt in one
piece each night in time for dinner and some
fine Asian beers. As I alluded to in an earlier
chapter, I nearly got squashed crossing the
freeway on one of my shortcut attempts.

My brother was able to accompany me into the
city on one occasion. We headed out in the
afternoon on the LRT and toured the downtown
commercial area of KL, as it's known by the
locals. Unfortunately we were unable to tour
the Petronas Towers, one of the largest
buildings in the world, because the tickets were
sold out. We settled instead for pictures
outside. We had to walk several blocks away
through dense motorcycle traffic in order to
capture the building through our cameras. After
I went home, my brother got the chance to check
out the Towers from the inside. Figures.

We ate at the Hard Rock Cafe (I know, I
know...A bit cheesy) and walked the meal off on
our way back to the LRT station, checking out
many bizarre characters all the way.

My backpack finally arrived in Kuala Lumpur,
just in time for me to leave. All right, maybe
two days before I left. Either way, I wound up
wearing my brother's clothes and buying some
nifty, high-dollar underwear in the Hyatt gift
shop.

Eventually, my tour in KL ended and I rode

the rails back to Singapore for my flight home. I met several intelligent, outstanding guys on the train and we traded time grilling each other about our homelands. Books are great, but there is just no substitute for the real thing. We discussed politics, race, religion...You name it. After all, we did have six hours to kill.

My new-found friends took time out to show me how to get back to the airport by spending $2 USD instead of the $25 USD I had spent on the cab ride coming in. The subway was definitely the way to go.

After eight long hours in the airport, I foggily went through customs, semi-forgetful of the pack of bubble gum in my pants pocket. I say semi-forgetful, because a side of me always wants to push things to the limit (like trying to smuggle illegal bubble gum through Singapore), while another side of me simply does not. Things were going right peachy until the woman wanded me down. Her instrument went off and my stomach dropped. I hoped I wasn't going to get caned for my heinous offense. Luckily, I got off with a dirty look, as I pulled the pack out and quickly shoved it back in. And believe me, they don't mess around in Singapore. Security is tight and they're all about business.

Heading east, I settled in for the hellacious flight back home, looking forward to gaining back that lost day in my life.

Pretty Pigs All in a Row

Arizona, 2003

Each February, a group of us city-dwellers
descend on the desert to hunt javelina. We call
them pigs, but they're actually overgrown
members of the rat family. You'd be hard
pressed to call them handsome, with their
bristly hair, long snouts and foul aroma. But
they sure are fun to hunt and if you cook them
right, they're good eatin' as well. Javelina
have a wide habitat area in Arizona, ranging
from the low deserts to the mountains. They
live in herds and although they can't see worth
a damn, they have an uncanny sense of smell.

We prefer to hunt the smelly critters in a
series of washes draining into the Hassayampa
River north of Phoenix. Rugged high-desert,
full of saguaro, prickly pear, cholla, yucca,
mesquite, palo verde, sagebrush, and ocotillo.
The javelina share the land with coyotes, mule
deer, rattlesnakes, jackrabbits, scorpions,
quail, tarantulas, fox, hawks, owls, and
unfortunately...Cows.

The weather in February can be temperamental
as hell. You might enjoy optimal conditions,
with clear, blue skies and 70-degree days, or
cold, rain-soaked, wind-blown conditions. And
then there are the hot-as-hell-conditions, where
hunting for any length of time can become
downright unbearable. Especially if you're
carrying a pig over your shoulder for several
miles back to camp.

The usual suspects arriving to hunt and
party each year include the Caraway clan (Bill,
Kevin, and Terry), Howard Hughes, Harry Doerr,
Matt Davis, Janet and Randy MacDonald, Jeff
Abraham, Greg Gallagher, and a whole host of

characters that join in on a year to year basis.
My cousin Pat Faith even flew in from Ohio a few
years back to participate. He's still telling
the stories. Although, I don't know which are
better, the hunting stories or the camp stories?

The beauty of pig hunting is the fact that
you don't have to wake up at the crack of dawn
to get into position like deer or elk hunting
(a.k.a. more time to party at night). You can
hunt pigs all day long. We generally get
started at around 8 a.m. and hunt until early
afternoon, after which we return to camp to
reenergize and take a break from the sun. By
late afternoon, we're back in the washes and
chasing pigs again. Half the fun is riding
quads and motorcycles up and down the main
washes in order to get to a suitable hunting
location. We can cover a huge area by riding to
the head of a drainage and then walking down.
Afterward, we can walk across a plateau, or what
we call "the flats", enabling us to hunt up a
different drainage on the way back to the bikes.

We hunt during a HAM (handgun, archery, and
muzzleloader) season, and most desire to carry
handguns or bows. I prefer my trusty old Colt
Anaconda, a stainless steel .44 caliber revolver
with a short four-inch barrel. Some of the guys
like to think I have barrel envy, just looking
at their eight-inch models, but you know the old
adage: "it's not how big it is, but how you use
it". At times, I feel like a participant in a
Wild West shootout, as a herd is spotted and
five or six guys are all plugging away at once.
Quite an adrenaline rush to say the least.

Javelina are tough little bastards that can
take a .44 slug and keep right on chugging. It
never ceases to amaze me. I can't imagine too
many humans taking a .44 slug in the hip and
continuing to run. When agitated, javelina
knash their teeth and the coarse hair on their
backs stand straight up.

Some years we have a lot of success and some
years we don't have much luck at all. I
remember returning to camp one year with five
pigs strapped to the back of my ATV. All five

in our party tagged out that afternoon. Then again, we've had years where eleven hunters left eleven tags unfilled. The drought here in the Southwest has really ravaged the herds and just about everything else as well. We're all praying for rain.

Although the hunt itself is awesome, camp life may be even better. We never fail to attract non-hunting friends from Phoenix, who make the journey up just to partake in the delicious orgies of deer, elk, antelope, quail, javelina, buffalo, rattlesnake, halibut, and of course...Alcohol. Festivities have included fire-jumping contests, where grown men jumped over bonfires, flames tickling their butts and a tiny slip away from sure disaster. Potatoes are annually launched from a tube out at unsuspecting would-be-crappers trying to do their business in the bushes. Gag gifts and fart machines. Horseshoes and chipping contests. And of course...Lots of hunting stories, some of them even factual. The fun never ends...Or at least not until we're forced to go home. Better than Disneyland any day!

The wives and girlfriends can thank the Arizona Game and Fish Department for pushing back the dates of the hunt by a week. The hunt traditionally fell on Valentine's Day, and didn't set well with some of the ladies. What's a guy to do? Buy some flowers early and get out to the desert to chase pigs around. I guess we could always invite the women...But then again...Nnnaaahhhh.

Have No Fear

Arizona, 2003

Fears. Everybody's got them, whether they
will admit to them or not. I'm not referring to
phobias, or irrational fears, such as the fear
of bologna sandwiches (which by the way, you
probably should be afraid of). For some, it may
be heights, for others, wide open spaces,
crowds, scissors, or dogs. Take the fear of
heights for instance. You may be deemed a bit
phobic if the thought of getting up on a three-
foot stepladder scares the living hell out of
you. On the other hand, I wouldn't consider you
phobic at all if you said crossing a wet, mossy
log spanning a thousand-foot chasm kind of
concerned you.

In other words, fears and phobias are very
relative. Take crowds for instance. Perhaps
the only people who truly, honestly dig tightly
packed spaces are perverted frotterists, who
cash in on the opportunity to rub up against
people in order to get their kicks. I mean, who
the hell honestly likes being jostled and
squished among bad breath and body odor.

My fear is tight places, or the sensation of
being stuck, with no clear way out. These fears
are really a bitch when they hamper me from
doing things that I love to do.

Like kayaking for instance. I'm not
hydrophobic...I don't fear water itself. Not
even turbulent, chaotic whitewater. O.K.,
there's a point where that can become pretty
scary as well. But that's rational.

My fears come to the surface when I'm not.
In other words, I begin to really feel
uncomfortable when I'm upside down in a rapid.
I know how to roll pretty well, but I always

seem to have trouble trying to convince myself to stay in my boat long enough to accomplish the task of rolling. My fears keep me from progressing in the sport. It's the reason why my friend Christian Bates, who is an excellent, fearless kayaker, keeps getting better, while I find myself preferring semi-retirement. I simply don't like being underwater in my kayak; I feel the need to escape. The need to be free. Unfortunately, in heavy, continuous whitewater, a swim can spell certain disaster and in extreme cases...Death.

I grew up around rivers and have been involved with whitewater since I was a little kid. My dad, Ed "Eddie" Quinn is a river rat from way back and showed us kids the ropes at an early age. He has also introduced plenty of others to the sport of whitewater and continues to do so.

My dad has had his own close calls and a very-near-death experience. While kayaking on a January afternoon in a swollen, frigid, Tonto Creek in Arizona, he took a very lengthy swim, eventually falling unconscious and succumbing to hypothermia. He'd be the first to tell you he had no business on the creek that day. The water level was way too high and the air temperatures were way too cold. He hasn't kayaked much since. I wouldn't call it a phobia, but more of a rational, traumatic experience, which keeps him from getting into the cockpit. He continues to be an avid whitewater rafter.

The feeling that you're about to drown is just no fun. Although I've flipped a raft or two in my day, I've never come closer, at least in my own mind, to drowning than when I was in a kayak. Thus, I have lingering issues every time I slide into my boat and head downstream.

I'll never forget stupidly flipping over at the top of Overboard Rapid on the Upper Salt River in Arizona. Separated from my boat, I swam downstream and headed right for a huge undercut rock. I closed my eyes right before impact, expecting my head to become crushed like a grape. Instead, I was yanked violently beneath the undercut rock and dragged like a rag doll to the bottom of the river. I recall the water getting darker and darker and thinking to myself...This is it, I'm going to die right here, right now. I even remember laughing as I was pulled down, because it all seemed so surreal, like I was outside of the situation looking in. I managed to swim back up to the light and pop my head up for air. Just as I did, I encountered another undercut rock, and was pulled violently down once more. This time not as far and not nearly as dark as the first yankdown. Which was fortunate, as I was just about out of oxygen. I swam up and somehow made it to the bank and waited for my kayak, which came floating nonchalantly down to me a few minutes later. My paddle ended up on some rocks on the opposite bank. It wasn't pretty and probably scarred my kayaking career for life. Today, I mainly prefer class III and under recreational runs in my kayak. I tend to prefer a raft for big water excursions.

My younger sister, Kristie Fassette, had a near-drowning experience on the Upper Salt River as well. She was sucked out of a raft while tackling Quartzsite Falls (prior to the falls' untimely demise at the hands of dynamite). She was recirculated in the reversal hole beneath the falls for what seemed like an eternity before reaching the surface for a brief, hopeful moment, only to be snatched again and taken for another terrifying underwater ride.

Fortunately, she's a strong swimmer and managed to pop back up to safety, unscathed physically, but definitely not emotionally. Her paddle danced upright on the water for a full twenty seconds! That fear is rational. Kristie's love of whitewater remains, although she's always visibly shaken when we approach Quartzsite, which is still somewhat intimidating even after being declawed by dynamite in the early 1990s.

Caving, or spelunking for you purists, is another sport in which I constantly must overcome my fear of tight spaces in order to survive. And I don't mean a walk down the path in a commercial cave with a raincoat on. I'm referring to wet, crawl-on-your-belly-type caves. I don't mind the dark, bats, or even the fear of being lost. It's the tight squeezes that bind me up...Quite literally. Becoming caught in a narrow crawl space. Your heart rate increases, causing your chest to expand. This of course results in your stuck body becoming even more stuck. It's quite a vicious circle. Eventually panic sets in, complicating matters even further.

I remember one of my first caving experiences on the Mogollon Rim in Arizona with a friend named Keith Lockwood in a hole named Pine Cave. Pine Cave is a tight, twisting little cave better suited for tall, lanky guys, than it is for short squatty guys like myself. We had a few beers prior to meeting up with an acquaintance of Keith's at the entrance. Beer and caves don't mix all that well. I can't recall the fellow's name, but he was an accomplished caver, even if he was a little wacky. I can still remember crawling around for what seemed like an eternity (probably only an hour or so, cave time being so unreal anyway), then turning off our flashlights to conserve the batteries while we rested. In the complete darkness and silence of the cave, the guy leaned very close and said "Jeff do you believe in God?". Now that's scary. His voice sounded almost ominous and I began wondering what was real and what wasn't. The hair on the back of my neck stood up. It was freaky. I never caved with that guy again.

In that same cave years later, while adventuring with Dusty Decarlo, I happened to get stuck in what we dubbed the *Winnie the Pooh Honeypot Spot*. It's really sort of a fulcrum point (almost teeter-tauterlike) where you have to propel yourself up an incline and through a tight spot between the roof and floor of the cave. Getting down through the spot was a hassle, but not that bad. The problem wasn't going downhill, where you had momentum; it was going uphill, with no momentum and nothing to push off of.

I'm a little bit wider than Dusty, so I usually went first through squeezes, figuring if I couldn't make it through, then we couldn't go any further anyway, as solo caving is absolutely brainless and stupid. So I tried my best to get up and through the opening, but ended up stuck in the middle. Dusty was behind me and therefore couldn't pull me out from the front, so I had to try and push off of his shoulder behind me. I just got more stuck. I started breathing more and more rapidly even as I told myself to be calm. Sweat beading all over my body, my chest expanding, I began to panic. I just wanted out. My arms only fit beneath my body, so they were of no use to me. I finally resorted to propelling myself forward, half-inch at a time, with my chin. I eventually managed to get through the spot and was able to laugh about the whole situation.

I guess that's enough said about fears.

The Rhino in Rome

Italy, 1997

Scammed. Nobody ever likes to be scammed and the only thing worse than being scammed is having to admit to the fact that you've been scammed. I've been very fortunate throughout my travels. Sure, I've paid too much for a cheap trinket here and there, but that's always been a matter of paying a few cents too much, and besides, I always knew the person I paid too much to needed the extra few cents more than I did. The only time I can truly recall being scammed through an honest con job (kind of an oxymoron) was in Rome.

Dusty Decarlo and I were walking back from the Vatican (no, we didn't see the Pope, and yes, I did sneak a few snapshots of the Sistine Chapel) along the Tiber River, unable to catch a ride on the bus, which constantly seemed to pass us by. We had purchased one of those hop on-hop off passes, but we hadn't been able to hop back on after hopping off at the Vatican that morning. Every time we saw our bus it was two hundred yards in front of us and on the move in the opposite direction.

It was a beautiful autumn day, leaves falling, people smiling, cats frolicking. After crossing the street, we ducked into a building, which houses the "laughing man" to snap a quick picture. The "laughing man" is a face on the wall that in theory anyway, is supposed to engulf a liar's hand when placed in its mouth. Unfortunately, a Japanese tour bus pulled up as we were arriving and mobbed the poor "laughing man", flashbulbs flashing, causing the overburdened "laughing man" to stop laughing.

Just as I thought I might get a clear shot

off, a woman pounced into the frame and stuck her hand in the old boy's mouth. You can imagine the first question asked when I break out the picture album..."Who the hell's that lady?". "My aunt", I tell them. "Oh".

Crossing several more streets, we made our way through an empty field, which used to contain the Circus Maximus. You could almost hear the chariots whirring by if you listened very closely. Or maybe that was a *Fiat*?

A car suddenly pulled up alongside us and asked for directions to the Vatican. Having just come from there, we gave the guy directions and he began pulling away. Then he hesitated and inquired if we were familiar with the name Pierre Cardin of Paris? Of course we had, and this led into a conversation in which he discussed his connection with the company as a traveling representative. This was *of course* the last stop on his trip and he had two leather coats remaining in his inventory, which he wanted to give to us at no cost.

We had absolutely no use for leather coats, but what the hell, if they were free, then bring 'em on. Then he proceeded to open up his trunk and show us the coats. One green one and one black one. Just as he was about to hand us the coats and take off, he said he was on his way back to Paris and needed some gas money. He wanted to know if we could help him out, since after all, he was giving us free coats. Of course Paris is a long way from Rome and gas prices what they are in Europe, he would require a small fortune to get there. He wanted some astronomical amount, but angrily settled for $30 USD apiece and sped off.

There we stood at the Circus Maximus, with our "pleather", as it turned out, coats. Coats that we didn't want, or have room for, to begin with. Ben Hur would have bagged on us for sure. The whole scam went down in less than two minutes. The guy was really slick; I have to hand it to him. Even though we were scammed, I have to imagine that he made very little off the deal, "pleather" or not. The coats were actually pretty nice. I'd never wear one, but pretty nice nevertheless. PETA would approve of them anyway. All we could do was shake our heads and laugh. And try and figure out what the hell to do with the coats.

We were backpacking our way through Europe and had been for some time, so our packs were already overburdened to say the least. We decided that we would hand them off to the first set of bums that we came across, which we figured wouldn't take too long in Rome.

Walking past the Coliseum, we found a row of artisans plying their trade on the street. Not exactly bums, but perhaps one step away. Some African carvings caught our eye and we asked the proprietor if he would be interested in trading a couple of carved animals for the coats. He misunderstood us at first and thought we were trying to sell him the coats. Finally we struck up a bargain using intricate hand signals and gestures. We handed over the coats in exchange for a carved rhino and a wild boar. He was selling the carved figures for a couple of dollars a piece, so he was really exuberant about the deal. Said he was trying to make enough money to return to Senegal. I hope he made it.

We took grinning pictures of ourselves holding the wooden figures. I'm sure passerby thought we were totally cracked.

We headed down the road to a small restaurant, where we ate pizza outside on a fumy sidewalk and watched poor bastards try and cross the street. I felt like I was inside the game Frogger, as pedestrians attempted to cross eight laneless rows of traffic in a system where the pedestrians have the right of way, but there aren't any crosswalks. Forward and backward, and then forward again. Bologna wagons bleating like sheep on the street. We thought the reason there were so many bologna wagons (ambulances) on the street must surely have something to do with the fat intake from all the sausage, but I guess it could have had something to do with the *Frogger* game as well?

At RockyGrass with the Jav

Colorado, 2003

Judging by the temperature (it stays hot as hell in Phoenix well into October), you'd never know it, but summer is almost over...At least for me anyway. Back to work. Playtime will have to wait, at least long enough for me to relocate to Cuzco, Peru, where I can open up a pizza shop and conduct history tours. Maybe search for lost cities in my spare time...Well perhaps someday, but not today. Today, I'll sit here at this confounded computer, listen to some David (The Dawg) Grisman and attempt to tell you about my experiences at the RockyGrass Bluegrass Festival in Lyons this past weekend.

I arrived home from an awesome kayaking trip on the Chama River in New Mexico, played a little soccer, drank a few beers, pawned my mongrel off on my ex-wife and boarded a plane to Denver.

I was headed to my first bluegrass festival. Yes, I was a virgin. I've been to many a music fest, but never to a three-day affair where I scarcely knew any of the tunes or performers. I was basically ignorant. But I wanted to learn.

My old friend John "Javelina Sours" Sweet picked me up from the airport and we headed down to his place in Colorado Springs. After sitting in on one of Jav's brilliant history lectures at Pike's Peak Community College, we hit a grocery store and headed north to the little town of Lyons, situated in the foothills northwest of Denver.

We found our designated campground in a park alongside St. Vrain Creek where softball fields were transformed into tent spaces and the place was filling up fast. Red sandstone walls stared steeply down to the clear creek below as Jav took time out to admire the scenery, exclaiming:

"Damn, there sure are a lot of nice looking...Tents around here".

Some of you may be wondering where Jav acquired his illustrious nickname? He actually had the name bestowed on him by me during a trip to Arizona quite awhile back. He flew into Tucson for some sort of a history or hound dog conference (can't remember which) and we hooked up for a few days of camping north of Tucson after his conference formalities ended.

We drove up to Oracle, where we knocked on doors in the rain searching for someone that knew Edward Abbey. Through a great stroke of luck, we found a woman that had known Abbey and she invited us in for an interview. Afterwards, she introduced us to a guy (the local mailman) that had film footage and several rare movies. So we sat around on his couch eating Doritos and watching vintage Abbey material for the rest of the overcast afternoon.

I know what you're thinking...What the hell does this have to do with a Javelina? Well, after the Oracle scene, we headed into the desert to camp for the night and right around dusk, while hiking along a hillside, a herd of pigs jumped up and Jav let one have it. We each ate about five pounds of meat around the fire, caveman style, with our hands, and Jav stuffed the remainder of the meat in his carry-on luggage and took it home with him to Colorado. I can just picture the look on the x-ray tech's face. From that day forward he was and continues to be known as...Jav Sours.

Back to Colorado. We set up Jav's tent (alongside the aforementioned plethora of beautiful tents) on that fine, warm July night and fell asleep to the sounds of mandolins and guitars carrying softly through the thin Rocky Mountain air.

In the morning we began what would become the routine for the next several days. After a trip to the porta-john, we headed to the creek for a cold, soap less, refreshing, creek bath. Since the powers-to-be weren't allowing charcoal grills and maybe better yet, because we forgot to bring a pan, we had to forgo the breakfast burritos, opting instead for a goat beer (cheap beer of any variety) and a vitamin.

We saddled up and walked over to the RockyGrass Bluegrass Festival, which was located in a beautiful valley along the St. Vrain River. The temperatures were above normal and we pretty much baked in the sun as we soaked in the music. Eventually clouds replaced the sun, as thunderous buildups climbed to the heavens above our tarp, chasing festivarians to cover on more than one occasion. But the music played on...Lightening or not.

The crowd was quite an eclectic mix and included grogans (Aussie slang for grubby unkempt sons of bitches), Denver yuppies complete with corporate logo lawn chairs and cooler cups, Old hippies with young children, amateur musicians who lived to play at night in camp, veteran festival goers and perhaps a few virgins like myself.

I was totally amazed by the civility and Karma displayed. I never witnessed a single fight or argument. There was virtually thousands of dollars sitting in tents at the campground each day, yet everyone, to my knowledge, lost nothing. You set up your tarp at the show, threw down your belongings and walked away to dance for hours without ever worrying that your stuff would be there when you returned. Pretty damn refreshing stuff in this grab all world we live in. Maybe that heathen devil weed aroma that filled the air was to blame for such a heinous occurrence? I must admit however that although everybody was peaceful, they weren't altogether friendly. It was a pretty typical Western crowd with their minds turned inward. Sorry, but that's the truth. And I'm a Westerner. Put it this way if we had been congregating in the Midwest somewhere, I'm sure people would have proven more friendly and less, as Jav says...Surly.

Every evening as the sun made its way westward and the shadows drew long, a trio of bighorn sheep made their way along the cliffs above the river, opposite the festival grounds. A white female basked on top of a backlit promenade every night, watching the stage intently for hours, digging what she witnessed.

After watching bluegrass greats like Del McCoury, Tony Rice, Peter Rowan, David Grisman, Mike Marshall, Vasser Clements, Herb Pederson, Tim O'Brien, and a whole host of others, the audience geared its self up for the transition from observer to participant. The campgrounds became ripe with "pickin' sessions", where the talented and untalented alike, strummed along beside one another all hours of the night. Several of the performing artists even managed to make there way to some of the "picks" in the main campground. Making music with their followers. Now that's really cool.

I found that many of the performers were happy to jump up on stage and play with other performers. So much so, that it became commonplace. Except that is for the Saturday night headliner, Ricky Scaggs, who invited no one up on stage and came off as a bit "Nashville corporate", according to Jav. Great musician and band, they just didn't seem to strike that cord with a lot of festivarians, who chose instead to make their way back to the campgrounds to play their own music.

One evening as I stood near the creek drinking one of the fine New Belgium Brewery beers, a self-professed local accosted me for some conversation. "Damn, I never seen so many ugly white women in one place in my whole life", the gentleman stated. He went on to tell me that everyone at the show had sandals and hats on and how ridiculous that was. I happened to have *Vans* on, so he thought I was all right, even if I did have a boony cap on. I asked him if maybe the fact that it was so incredibly sunny and the fact that the creek was so incredibly inviting had anything to do with the choice of attire by the festivarians. "Hell, I don't know dude, I just know there's a whole lot of ugly women around here." I probably don't have to tell you that the gentleman himself was no peach. And his buddy that crept out of the bushes a moment later looked sort of like a troll but still managed to echo the sentiments of his friend.

Moments later, Lyons resident number one said he was going home. "I got drugs and when I got drugs my old lady's clothes just fall off." And then some sage advice for the troll: "Dude you got no chance here, you might as well go home, you ain't got no drugs and how in the hell you supposed to get together with one of these hogs without any drugs?" "I don't know, I guess you're right dude, maybe I ought a just go home", replied the troll. Oh how our vanity overlooks our own mirror.

On the last afternoon of the festival we met two women we dubbed the Ying-Yang sisters from Denver. Ann Marie was blue-eyed and blonde, while Sue possessed dark features. They were interested in traveling and drinking beer, so I bored them with tales of travel in between Blue Paddle Pilsners. Jav was with us initially but drifted away to the stage, leaving me to my own devices. The Ying-Yang sisters and I danced together amongst the tiki torches, managing to break my beer cup, but fortunately, no bones in the process. Later on we relaxed beneath a pair of gigantic oak trees and watched the encore and the sheep. Unfortunately, the show ended and the two girls kissed me on the cheek and headed abruptly to the shuttle bus, leaving me no trace of their existence. Such is life. Such is life.

Jav and I retired to the camp and cooked some brats on an illegal barbeque grill in the drizzling rain and reflected on the show and life in general. Wondering what the hell it's all really about. Perhaps someday I'll figure it all out...Or then again...I won't.

Final Comment

Congratulations, you somehow made it through this beat, crummy book of mine (unless of course you're cheating and this is the first page that you've read). Or maybe the only page you're going to read. I'm afraid I'll never measure up to any of my literary heroes such as John Steinbeck, Edward Abbey, Jack Kerouac, Robert Young Pelton, Tim Cahill, or P.J. O'Rourke. But damn, it sure would be nice to travel and write books for a living...

If you have any corrections, criticisms, questions or comments please feel free to e-mail me at **manonthescene2003@hotmail.com**. Also, if anyone out there has been to some really cool destinations and wants to share, please have at it. I'm always looking for information (and deals) on new places to explore. I'm always looking forward to meeting new people on the road. Perhaps a **Man on the Scene** get together in some far off, crazy locale is in order? Take care and may all your adventures be good ones. Thanks, JQ